Praise for *Achievable*

"A refreshingly simple, yet profoundly impactful, approach to leadership. *Achievable* is concise, engaging, and filled with relatable stories. It will be a go-to resource for any aspiring leader." —Capt. Michael Abrashoff, Author, *It's Your Ship*

"Fraser's focus on engaging, enabling, and empowering Chartwell's long-term care team was instrumental in increasing employee engagement and resident satisfaction survey results in our long-term care division. It also positioned the team to effectively and courageously meet the many challenges that we faced throughout the pandemic." —Karen Sullivan, President and Chief Operating Officer, Chartwell Retirement Residences

"*Achievable* is a must read for leaders who want to engage team members, increase retention, and improve performance. I found it to be inspiring, motivational, and packed with relatable stories that can be easily implemented. It should be the next read for any leader looking to drive change." —John Scotland, Chief Executive Officer, Steeves and Rozema Group

"I first met Fraser early in his CEO days, and when we discussed leadership practices, I described him as a 'sponge,' constantly listening to and absorbing ideas from everywhere and everyone. In *Achievable,* Fraser demonstrates how he transformed the best of many leadership approaches to *achieve* remarkable outcomes at all levels of long-term care—and even through the pandemic! *Achievable* is an incredible resource for anyone looking for a practical, straightforward, and no-nonsense approach to honing their leadership skills, overcoming the challenges of 'too much to do,' and helping others to be all they can be. A quick read that might be the best two hours of your leadership journey." —Ron Martyn, Co-owner, Silver Meridian

"A fantastic read and practical guide for any leader that is looking for the 'secret' to fostering a high-performance organization." —Brent Gingerich, Chairman and CEO, peopleCare Communities

"*Achievable* is a simple but powerful message to all leaders that it is our kindness, compassion, and individuality that truly make magic each and every day. Leadership is not about being the smartest person in the room but instead about our ability to get the most out of each and every person in the room." —Shawn Riel, COO, Omni Quality Living

"An engaged team delivers better outcomes. *Achievable* reminds us of the importance of acknowledging work done well by our people, as opposed to focusing only on areas needing improvement. It's a simple and powerful way to increase engagement and impact the lives of team members and leaders in any sector, including health care." —Salimah Walji-Shivji, Chief Operating Officer and General Counsel, AgeCare

"Fraser Wilson illuminates a simple truth that we, as leaders, intrinsically understand but frequently don't act upon: success comes through engaging, enabling, and empowering our people. Through his easy to understand and implement People First approach, he shows us how to unleash the potential in our teams to achieve outstanding results. The most wonderful part of his story is that, in addition to improving organizational performance, it also creates a more rewarding and joyful—indeed, 'life-giving'—experience for everyone." —James Schlegel, CEO, Schlegel Villages

"*Achievable* is your playbook to a more intentional, well-designed, and relational approach to leadership, creating results with your people, through passion and potential. Fraser's practical approach together with proven results and heartfelt stories will inspire you to engage, enable, and empower your people." —Deborah Bakti, Author, *Now What?*

"*Achievable* perfectly embodies the spirit and successes of Fraser Wilson. It is written as Fraser speaks: humbly confident and evangelical in his belief in the power of people. He understands why we may not always practice his people first philosophy, but gently reminds us of the possibilities of what will happen when we do. It's a warm bath and a bucket of cold water all at once. *Achievable* will be a must read for leadership teams and those who wish to lead within organizations." —Don MacKay, CEO, Align Home Health Care

"*Achievable* convincingly reminds leaders that they have their greatest impact when they are with their people, not managing paperwork. It lays out an effective engagement solution that puts people first, honours their contribution, and engages them in a better, brighter future." —Ryan Bell, CEO, Southbridge Care Homes

"I've known Fraser and his approach to leadership for years. He understands the important role that his people play in the delivery of service to his residents. He put his people first, inspired them with a higher purpose, and invested in their skills and knowledge. He enabled them to live into their potential. *Achievable* is a short and easy read that's sure to improve engagement levels for leaders and team members alike." —Jayne Harvey, CEO and Owner, FCS International

"*Achievable* has captured the essence of organizational leadership and personal relationship building through clear, relatable stories and strategies that are sure to lift employee engagement levels and improve performance outcomes." —Dan Kaniuk, CEO, Responsive Management Inc.

Achievable

A Simple and Proven Way to Create a Culture of Possibility and Potential

Fraser Wilson

B·ALL·U·CAN·B PUBLICATIONS

Some names and identifying details have been changed to protect the privacy of individuals.

Published by BALLUCANB Publications, Bethany, Ontario
www.achievableculture.com

GIRL FRIDAY PRODUCTIONS

Edited and designed by Girl Friday Productions
www.girlfridayproductions.com

Cover design: Paul Barrett and Ainsley Gabbani
Project management: Mari Kesselring
Editorial production: Katherine Richards

ISBN (paperback): 978-1-7380006-0-9
ISBN (ebook): 978-1-7380006-1-6

First edition

To the leaders and team members in all long-term care departments, you inspire me with your commitment, dedication, love, and compassion for your residents. You are remarkable and truly make a meaningful difference in the lives of others.

Contents

Introduction

Here's the blunt truth. The only thing, I mean, the one and only thing, that determines the success of any business is *people*. Full stop. Period. That's it.

Sure, there are all kinds of other things that affect business success. The mission and vision matter. Strategy and market positioning have a bearing on it. It's not possible without strong sales. Product quality, usability, and effectiveness factor in. But the single greatest impact is made by people.

It's bewildering to me that so many businesses and their leaders are still "profit first" focused. They concentrate their time and attention on sales, strategies, and statistics. They inundate their leaders with follow-up, analysis, and reports. They ask them to do more, to work harder, and so few take the time to recognize and appreciate their efforts. And they wonder why they can't get ahead or make progress.

They must believe that, by prioritizing profit over their people, they'll be more successful. It's simply not true. They're unintentionally limiting their potential, their people, and their performance by doing so.

What is true is that when companies put their People First, honour and respect their contributions, invest in their skills and knowledge, and empower them to deliver exceptional experiences, those companies become more successful, improve performance, and make more money.

According to Gallup, only 21 percent of employees are engaged at work in Canada. Globally the average increased from 22 to 23 percent for the first time in years. But it's still only 23 percent!

In Canada two-thirds of the workforce is quietly quitting. Globally the average is 59 percent. People are no longer willing to do more or work harder. They're doing the minimum to get by or looking for employment elsewhere.

Regardless of how you look at these statistics, engagement levels worldwide are unnecessarily low.

It doesn't need to be that way.

Like you, your people need to be seen and heard, to be informed and included. They long for the opportunity to grow, to be better, to make a meaningful impact. When you take time to be with your people, to show them that you care, that you value them, you'll be well on your way to raising the levels of engagement and the success of your business.

When your people feel appreciated, they'll do more, work harder, take more initiative, and improve performance.

In fact, according to Gallup, workplaces with engagement levels greater than 70 percent experience a 23 percent increase in profits.

It literally pays to engage your people.

Intuitively, you know this. You know the means to your success is with your people. They're the ones who connect with your customers, build relationships, deliver experiences, and drive sales. Working with respect and appreciation, in harmony and cohesion, you know you can achieve incredible things together.

Yet, despite your desire and internal drive to create a culture of possibility and potential, you feel pulled in multiple directions. The demands on you are immense and intense. So much so, you struggle to see beyond your daily demands and challenges. You're likely tied to your desk, busy being busy—you log countless hours and never seem to get on top of that mountain of paperwork.

The consequence: all these demands pull you away from your people. They feel underappreciated, unimportant, just like another cog in the wheel. They're becoming resigned and disengaged and doing the minimum to get by. This isn't what you want.

Achievable answers the call of leaders looking for an effective engagement solution. It lays out a simple and proven way to create a culture of possibility and potential.

Achievable puts People First. That's the foundation of the book. It's a solution that will move the needle on the disengagement epidemic.

The strategies used in *Achievable* are not based on research and academia. There are no fancy theories or philosophies. This book doesn't inundate you with multiple tasks to do, and you don't need a masterclass to implement its teachings.

They're just simple, understandable, doable people strategies that honour team members, tap their potential, increase performance, and improve profitability.

Achievable inspires by example. It's a call to action. An invitation to do things differently—one that's only limited by your dreams and aspirations.

Many have taken this path before you and are the better for it. They took small steps and applied them consistently, building their confidence and credibility as they went.

Whether you're leading an organization or a department within one, *Achievable* will enable you to rise above your daily demands and challenges and demonstrate what's possible when you engage, enable, and empower your people.

Believe me, when you commit to the steps laid out in this book, it'll pay you back time and time again.

FINDING FAULT BE DAMNED

I've spent twenty-five years leading long-term care (LTC) organizations in Ontario. I've lived through the sector's highs and lows, its constraints and challenges. It's heavily regulated, underfunded, over-scrutinized, and chastised by the media. It's a sector fixated on finding fault.

In my earlier years I was owner and CEO of OMNI Health Care. We had sixteen LTC homes and fifteen hundred team members. We, too, were focused on finding fault and pursuing perfect compliance. Our leaders and managers would spend countless hours conducting audits, identifying areas for improvement, and creating action plans to resolve them. Seldom did we have time to fix deficiencies before facing yet another round of audits. We fell into a perpetual cycle of auditing, with little to show for our efforts.

We were unknowingly, and naively, doing this at our team members' expense. Instead of giving them credit for their good work, we focused only on the work they didn't do perfectly. Not exactly an engaging or appreciative workplace! And it certainly was not one that motivated anyone to go above and beyond.

The result: our performance was mediocre. I was discouraged and disappointed, as were our people. There had to be a better way.

If you're anything like me, and I believe you are, you'll never be comfortable with mediocrity—working tirelessly only to achieve average outcomes. It's soul-sucking. It depletes your energy, dampens your enthusiasm, lessens your drive, and limits your life.

I wanted and needed more for me, my leaders, and our people. I knew we could do better. We had to get off the proverbial hamster wheel and do things differently.

I began to transition OMNI to a People First company. Our people became our priority. Everything we did, any new initiatives, had them in mind.

And we got better. Much better. OMNI became a premier LTC provider in Ontario. In fact, we had the best compliance records among Ontario's large organizations when the Ministry of Health first publicized the results. We demonstrated what was possible when you put People First and align them with supporting strategies.

After OMNI, I joined Chartwell Retirement Residences as vice president of Long-Term Care Operations. Chartwell is Canada's largest senior-housing operator, with two hundred retirement residences and LTC homes across the country. I was responsible for the twenty-seven LTC homes they owned and operated in Ontario.

What made this role different for me was that I would be leading a department within a very large organization. My influence was more restricted than when I had full autonomy as owner and CEO at OMNI, but as I'll show you, you can lead change and achieve incredible outcomes from within a division or department of a larger company.

The LTC platform comprised five thousand of Chartwell's fifteen thousand employees. That's one-third of all employees, yet we only represented twenty-seven of two hundred homes. We cared for thirty-three hundred residents, plus their families. That's a lot of personalities. Almost every home was unionized. We had more than fifty collective agreements, essentially two for each home.

We had more rules than NASA, or it certainly felt like it. Frequent inspections by the Ministry of Health were focused almost solely on either finding fault or noncompliance, with nearly six hundred rules and regulations. In fact, our sector was the only one where all we could do was "fail" in the eyes of the ministry (e.g., "the operator 'failed' to provide care in accordance with the care plan"). They spent little time acknowledging any new initiatives or progress being made in our homes or by our people.

Needless to say, the operating circumstances were arduous.

When I assumed my role, our homes were in good standing with the ministry and our performance met corporate expectations. We had a strong foundation on which to build. Although our administrators and managers met expectations, they were buried with internal and external reporting and never-ending tasks. They struggled to rise above these circumstances to spend the time needed to build rapport, connection, and community with their people.

As with OMNI, I changed their focus to put People First. We engaged the hearts and minds of our people by focusing on, and acknowledging, work done well. We inspired our people with a higher purpose and changed the way we led.

Through the strategies laid out in *Achievable,* we engaged, enabled, and empowered our leaders and team members to live into their potential. We became the platform that was leading change and demonstrating what was possible within the organization. It was life-giving. Fuel for our souls. It ignited our passion, lifted our spirits, and left us feeling more fulfilled knowing we were making a meaningful difference. It was a beautiful way to live and work, for everyone.

And you can have this too.

I have a deep desire to improve the lives of leaders and frontline team members. I wrote this book to Make Others More. To enable leaders like you to live better lives, love your work, and embrace the best in your people. I wrote it to inspire hope for a brighter future—one where you overcome the disengagement epidemic and create a culture of possibility and potential.

CHAPTER 1

People First

Success in business is all about people, people, people. Whatever industry a company is in, its employees are its biggest competitive advantage.

—Sir Richard Branson

It doesn't matter if you're in hospitality, health care, government, or environmental services. Exceptional customer experiences aren't delivered by products—they're created by people. Engaged, passionate, competent people, who are supported and encouraged to care deeply about how they serve. Whether you're buying a car, going out for a meal, staying in a hotel, or arranging care for a loved one, your experience depends on those who serve.

I was never a smart kid—I was very average, actually—and I have dyslexia to boot. It was my dad who saw potential in me. He was an entrepreneur, an accountant, a numbers guy. I was brought up in finance, and I have an economics degree. I spent the first years of my career learning OMNI's financial systems and developing budgets. As I grew in the business, I wanted to expand my understanding of it. I took a greater interest in operations. It was here that I discovered my passion for people. I felt most alive when I was with them. It was here that I came to understand that people, not numbers, were the means to a successful business. People were at the centre of everything we did, and they are for you too.

Frustrated by our compliance-preoccupied rinse-and-repeat cycle, I needed to find a better way to improve our performance. Driven and curious, I wanted to learn as much as I could about the culture in successful companies and how to replicate their practices.

I began to read leadership books and attend conferences on culture and change management. Book after book, conference after conference, there it was in neon lights: "PUT YOUR PEOPLE FIRST." The great companies were the ones that valued their people. Ritz-Carlton, Whole Foods, Home Depot, Southwest Airlines, Costco—they far outperformed their profit-first competitors. Those that didn't prioritize their people did so at their peril. They limited their potential, their performance, and, ironically, their very profitability.

I had found the wisdom and answers I needed.

The concept of People First was reaffirming and hopeful. People would become front and centre in all that we did. I created my personal motto: Making Others More. I wanted to create opportunities for our people to grow, to be better, to be all they could be. I needed them to know that they mattered, that they made a difference.

Achievable is dedicated to putting People First. That's the theme that runs throughout the book. It's laid out in a progressive sequence. Think of it as concentric circles starting with People First at its centre. Each circle, each chapter, building on the one before. Each one growing your confidence and credibility and broadening your leadership impact. Each step tapping the potential of your people, taking you closer to a brighter, more purposeful, more prosperous future for everyone.

The title of this book is *Achievable* for a reason. It is doable. When you change your focus from the busywork and the paperwork to prioritizing your people, you'll open up a whole new realm of possibilities for yourself and your people.

You'll take your initial steps toward People First by engaging the hearts and minds of your people by focusing on, and acknowledging, work done well. It will be the easiest, most gratifying step for you and your people. It's so important, it's the subject of the next chapter and a foundational step in the entire process.

You'll learn how this process worked, where we encouraged our leaders to make time to be present with their people, to build relationships and show appreciation for their work, and to acknowledge the difference they made each and every day.

From there, you'll inspire your people with a higher purpose and aspirational goals. At OMNI we introduced a new mission, and at Chartwell we revitalised the existing mission and brought it back to life. It was the higher purpose we were striving for. We infused it into our conversations and meetings. I emphasized it in my road shows to the homes, in conferences, and at leadership summits. It became ever present and top of mind for our leaders and team members. They would be the ones bringing it to life. We made our mission matter to everyone.

We then introduced aspirational goals to further define our mission and outline what our people would need to do to deliver on it. We encouraged each of our LTC homes to think beyond mere compliance and come up with projects or initiatives that aligned with those aspirational goals. And they did. Every home, without exception, had new initiatives. It was the work they wanted to do. The work they loved to do.

Next you'll make the transition from managing to leading by embracing the 3 *E*'s of People First leadership.

We taught our leaders how to *engage, enable,* and *empower* their team members, tap their potential, and demonstrate what's possible when you bring out the best in them. We engaged our people by inspiring and persuading them to do things differently. We let them know the reason for the change and explained how it would make their lives better.

We invested in their skills and knowledge. We developed our own dementia strategy and called it IMAGINE . . . Living Life to Your Potential. In the first year and a half we graduated 750 frontline team members from four days of training off-site. They returned to their homes reinvigorated and empowered to do things differently, to do them better, for our residents and each other.

And our compliance got better too! Why? Because our people were more engaged and empowered. They found greater joy and purpose in their work. They were more present and attentive to regulatory processes and expectations. "What gets rewarded gets repeated," the saying goes, and repeated it was, over and over again.

From here you'll delve into people-focused communication and uncover ways to provide your people with information they need to know, want to know, and like to know. During COVID-19 we used Team Ups on every shift, on every resident neighbourhood, to keep our people informed. These were fifteen-to-twenty-minute standing meetings that included all team members from all departments serving on those neighbourhoods. We discussed new protocols, shared updates on the health of our residents, and heard the apprehension and anxiety of our team members, and we acknowledged those who were going above and beyond. Our people had never felt more informed, heard, and included.

And we'll explore ways to overcome resistance, much of which will have diminished by the time you get there. We specifically encouraged our leaders to spend more time and attention on those team members who were doing good work and making a meaningful difference, not those who were resisting change. We would build our base of support this way. With each step and new initiative, we converted those who were sitting on the fence, as well as those resisting change. Once they saw that the new direction and practices achieved better outcomes, they would become willing participants in the new direction. Most would become believers.

At Chartwell, in two short years, we were acknowledged within the organization and the sector for achieving the seemingly impossible. We increased our resident satisfaction survey "very satisfied" score by 15 percent. We witnessed an increase of 7.5 percent in the "very engaged" score for employee engagement, where the corporate expectation was 2 percent for the same period. We bettered the provincial average with ministry inspection outcomes and quality indicators. And we were winning awards, internally and externally. Suffice to say, what started with small steps became a landslide of accomplishments. And it all began by engaging our people's hearts and minds by focusing on, and acknowledging, their work done well.

Each one of these steps puts your People First. When you keep them front and centre, and prioritized above all else, your life—and the lives of those you lead—will be better. You'll tap their potential and blaze a trail of new initiatives, creativity, and possibility. All you need to do is apply these steps consistently and persistently, with passion and enthusiasm, and you too can accomplish exceptional outcomes with your people.

A bright and prosperous future is yours for the taking.

CHAPTER 2

Focus On Work Done Well

I've learned that people will forget what you said, people will forget what you did, but people will never forget how you made them feel.

—Maya Angelou

You became a leader to do the work you love. To make a difference. To lead your people. To be the one who connects with and walks beside your people. You want to implement new initiatives, ones that engage your people and move you forward.

Achievable

Your gut is telling you that your people are ready for change. They need a better work environment. They need you. They long for your leadership, your passion and enthusiasm. They need you to put People First and acknowledge their good work.

But how to make the time? You're already doing so much. And you don't know that you have it in you to find more time. The difference here is how you choose to use that time. It's not more busywork time. Not more paper time. It's dedicated people time. It's "putting People First" time. And it's time that will pay you back over and over again.

PUTTING PEOPLE FIRST IS EASIER THAN YOU THINK

- *When you make time for your people, they'll notice.*
- *Take time to acknowledge their work, and they'll appreciate you.*
- *Do it consistently, and you'll lift the spirit in the workplace, and yours too.*

I had been at Chartwell for five months. During that time, I'd held three regional leadership summits. I asked our leaders if they believed that their people came to work with the intention to do good work. They responded with a resounding yes. I asked each table to give me a percentage for the work done well by their people. In each of the summits, comprising a total of twenty-seven teams, the response was between 85 and 90 percent.

Let's think about that, 85 to 90 percent: that's no passing grade. It's exceptional, an A grade. Whenever I received an 85 or higher in school, I was over the moon. The vast majority of the work done by our people was done really well!

Yet most of this work went unrecognized and underappreciated.

Our leaders conceded that most of their time and attention was spent on pushing paperwork, pursuing perfect compliance, and fixating on what wasn't working. What a missed opportunity! They agreed they had taken good work for granted.

What might happen, I asked, if they acknowledged work done well instead of merely looking for fault? How might their people feel? What would happen to the engagement levels in their homes? And what impact would this new approach have on their quality of work? I had them take ten minutes to discuss at their tables. The room began buzzing—faces and hands animated, light bulbs turning on in the minds of our people throughout the space. Their smiles and excitement said it all.

Once time was up, they responded with enthusiasm, saying, "My people would appreciate the acknowledgment." They said, "Team members would become more engaged." And the biggest realization: "The quality of their work would increase beyond 85 and 90 percent."

There it was. Cha-ching! The penny dropped. Aha moments were happening everywhere. By simply changing their focus to acknowledge work done well, they knew there would be a positive return on their time with and attention to their people.

Just as I had earlier, our leaders came to realize that their people did really good work. Work that we had been blind to. We had taken our people for granted, because we were always focused on fault and what they didn't do perfectly, as opposed to looking for and acknowledging the work they did well. This change, from chasing fault and perfect compliance to appreciating the incredible work that was already being done, was the spark that made all other progress possible.

This simple act of acknowledging work done well was the show of respect and appreciation that was missing with our practices. When our leaders started looking for the good, it was there in abundance. The more they acknowledged their people, the more engaged they became, the more initiatives they undertook, and the greater the progress they made.

This can be your story too.

WHERE FOCUS GOES, ENERGY FLOWS

Our leaders wanted to create a culture of possibility and

potential—those summits made that clear. But like many of us, they had struggled to see beyond daily demands and challenges.

There's no doubt, some paperwork does need to be addressed, compliance is important, and fixing what's broken is necessary. It shouldn't be at the expense of meaningful, people-centred progress. But it was. It shouldn't consume the vast majority of their focus and energy. But it did. It was the rut that our people were stuck in, one they couldn't get out of.

The summits were the beginning of our emergence from that rut and its path toward achieving exceptional outcomes. And origins of that progress are rooted in a simple concept: make the time to change your perspective from looking for fault to recognizing and acknowledging work done well by your people.

The reality is you're still going to be busy. You'll still have to balance people, paper, and processes. That was certainly the case for me, my team, and our administrators. Prioritizing your people is the single greatest factor that will enable you to "get out of the rut" and start making a meaningful difference in the lives of your people and your performance.

When you prioritize people over paperwork, beautiful things begin to happen. Like you, I appreciate being acknowledged for the work I've done. That's no different for your team. When they feel appreciated and respected, they'll do more, try harder, be more attentive, and complain less. Sales, customer satisfaction, and productivity increase. Absenteeism goes down. Grievances subside. Your load lightens, your energy renews, the future looks brighter, and you get to do more of the work you love.

And that mountain of paperwork? It gets smaller too. Why? Think about how much of it is generated by disenfranchised team members and unhappy customers, budget concerns, and missed sales targets.

Simply put, when your people are engaged, your performance improves.

FROM DISCIPLINE TO PEOPLE FIRST

Dany had been the director of care at one of our smaller homes for ten years. He was competent and led the home's largest department. When personnel issues arose, he would play "good cop, bad cop" with his administrator. Dany was always the bad cop, the de facto disciplinarian.

When the administrator retired, Dany had the opportunity to step up and lead the home. Before he applied for the position, he reached out to me for advice and mentorship. He was concerned that his prior role as bad cop would create an adverse perception of his leadership. I agreed that it would, and that if he continued to lead with a focus on finding fault and pursuing discipline, he would lose his people. They would become disgruntled, file grievances, and resist his direction, and operational performance would suffer. Worse, these issues would consume more of his time and attention.

Dany was on point. He read his situation well and understood the ramifications. We went through a number of strategies: focusing on acknowledging work done well, telling his team about his vision of the future, imagining what they could accomplish together. I encouraged him to share stories and celebrate the successes of those taking initiative and improving the lives of residents and team members.

To Dany's credit, he acted on the strategies. He was a sponge for knowledge. He read the books I recommended. He made time to be with his people and acknowledge their good work. He shared his vision of what they could accomplish together and shared stories of those taking initiative and implementing new practices.

He and his team introduced beer nights on Fridays, as well as wine with lunch on Sundays, and started leadership training with registered staff. Together they shared supportive techniques for residents living with dementia and created new evening programming for residents, just to name a few new initiatives. Dany's home became one of our best performers in his region and set new benchmarks for satisfaction survey results.

Dany understood the changes we were pursuing. He followed suit and chose to turn his focus and direct more energy toward his people, starting with acknowledging work done well. He was able to engage his people, drive new initiatives, and lift everyone's spirits, including his own.

BE INTENTIONAL

Lori, the administrator for one of our rural homes in Ontario, had become familiar with how I would start a meeting by asking the leader what they and their people were doing well.

When I went to visit Lori and her team, it was immediately clear to me that they were well prepared. They had assembled their stories. They were abundant, colourful, and uplifting.

Mary, I was told, was a new resident who had made an incredible transition. When she first moved into the home, she was reserved and withdrawn. She was always looking down and avoiding eye contact. She relied on our team members for all her care needs. Gradually, with the encouragement and kindness of team members, Mary became more confident in her new surroundings and more independent in her daily activities. Better still, she joined fellow quilters, made duvets, and became the home's greatest ambassador. She transitioned to living her life fully.

Gwen was nearing the end of life. It was estimated that she had one week to live. When our team asked her if there was anything they could do for her or anything special she would like to eat, she said, "I'd like an onion sandwich." As requested, the kitchen prepared one. To this day, they've never figured out the magic powers hidden in that onion sandwich! But for Gwen it was a true gift (with additional support from our physiotherapist and recreational team). She sprung back to life, to the joy of our team and her family. She returned to her social-butterfly self and never put down the phone.

I learned, too, that the residents' council wanted residents to sit on the home's recruitment committee. They wanted a say in the hiring process. The leadership team embraced this idea with open arms. It was a huge success. By all measures, the residents added value to the process. Interviewees especially appreciated the progressive idea. In fact, for many, it was why they chose our home as their place of employment.

Lori and the leadership team gave me many more examples that day. Clearly, they were proud of their accomplishments. "It was good for us to reflect on these stories," Lori said toward the end of the meeting. "We all needed a lift."

As I've outlined earlier, the work in long-term care is busy, and at times overwhelming. But even those who are doing great work, like Lori and her team, need to take time to focus on and acknowledge their good work. They certainly benefitted from it, and so can you.

When you meet with your people, be intentional and make it known what stories you're looking for: examples of exceptional customer service, a team member exercising patience and leaning in to understand a customer's questions, team members working in harmony, living the organization's values, or trying something new. Alternatively, you can do as I did and ask them, generally, what they're doing well. If you choose this route, be sure to ask for examples that align with your higher purpose and aspirational goals. Either way, they'll appreciate the time you made to be with them and the interest you took in their work.

BIG OPS: ANNUAL APPRECIATION CELEBRATION

Once a year, close to the holiday season, I would get together with my leadership team of twenty-five people. We called this Big Ops, a name I carried over from my OMNI days. We would reflect on our accomplishments for the year and review our goals for the next. I'd ask everyone beforehand to prepare a list of personal accomplishments they'd completed or worked on throughout the year.

These meetings were magical. After each person's presentation, their peers would remind them of other initiatives they had forgotten to mention or had been an active participant in. Better still, they spoke appreciatively about each other's character, how they were available to support others: how they were fully present, gentle, and encouraging, or stood strong when they had to. One person after the other, complimenting their colleague for the work they did and the way they did it.

We learned that Sarah took dementia training on her own accord and led the class with an average grade over 98 percent. Carey re-created our assessment tool and helped many of her colleagues with tech support. Sylvie put on her scrubs and "lived a day in the life of our staff" in three homes. Barb sat on a multitude of committees, and Steve participated in the redesign and financial modelling of our new homes. And Lisa helped lead the transition to a new pharmacy and oversee infection-control practices, and our immunization challenge. These are but a sampling of our team's initiatives.

It was awe-inspiring and an incredible way to end the year together.

As much as you think you know your people and what they do, this experience will tell you otherwise. Until you're living in their shoes, you can't really know. But this annual exercise can give you and your teammates a glimpse into the significance of their contributions.

If you want your People First strategy to succeed, start by acknowledging work done well. And if you want to end your year on a high note, go through this exercise. You'll all leave feeling appreciated, proud, and inspired.

CHAPTER 3

Your Presence Matters

Fraser has a personal awareness when he comes in the home. He makes it a point to acknowledge people, know names, and he makes people feel like they are the most important person in the room.

—The team at Chartwell Gibson

Your presence matters. It matters to your team.

You feel pulled in many directions and have so little time left for anything else. I get it. I agree it's a balancing act. But frankly, you can't create the culture you want by sitting behind your desk.

When you show your team that you care, that you're interested, that you value them, you'll be taking the first steps toward building the culture you desire.

When your people feel appreciated, their focus, and yours, becomes that of the aspirational goals and making progress toward them, not petty grievances. So, although it will take time initially, the benefits will start to accumulate, as will your personal satisfaction and sense of fulfilment.

To make the point, I'll contrast two leaders. Candace, who has become one of our foremost LTC leaders, stands as a symbol of the influence of presence. She came from humble beginnings, starting her career as a frontline personal support worker (PSW). While in that position she was elected union steward, then eventually the chief steward for one of our homes. Both the union and the home recognized Candace's leadership ability to know, understand, and represent the best interests of the membership.

Candace subsequently became the home's office manager and was often called on to be a mentor to other office managers. A student of lifelong learning and driven to be more, Candace became certified as an LTC administrator. She also enrolled in Chartwell's Aspiring Leaders program and before graduating was offered, and accepted, a role of administrator at one of our homes.

Within her first year, she led her team to win the Centre of Excellence for Long-Term Care within the company and was awarded the Ontario Long Term Care Association Home of the Year—exceptional accomplishments within such a short time.

Candace succeeded because of her presence—she knew how to relate to, connect with, and understand her people. She'd been in their shoes, and she was out on the floor looking for and acknowledging their work. During the pandemic she was known to put on her scrubs, pick up their duties, and work alongside them.

At the other end of the spectrum was a seasoned administrator with more than thirty years of experience. She may have been more active with her people in prior years, but her later years were served trying to lead from her desk, with limited visibility to families and her team alike. Whereas Candace was building relationships, respect, and synergy with her team, winning awards and demonstrating what is possible, this administrator's performance was regressing and her relationships deteriorating. The reality is, the more removed she became, the more concerns, grievances, and investigations she had to contend with. She was inundated with paperwork and problems.

In stark contrast, the more Candace embraced and connected with her people, the fewer concerns she had to address, the more successful and fulfilled she and her team became. Pride and belonging under her leadership were at all-time highs. She demonstrated that her presence mattered and that being at one with her people made the difference.

As another example, I had the opportunity to attend an event in the summer of 2023. I had a conversation with the CEO of a nonprofit organization. She told me that she had started conducting post-pandemic "stay meetings" with her people as opposed to waiting for exit interviews once they had left the organization. She wanted to know what she could do to entice them to stay and continue their careers with her.

They told her that they would appreciate opportunities to grow and enhance their skills and knowledge. They hoped to advance their careers with time and experience.

When she asked them what else she could do to support them, they said, "Continue to be present on the floors. It matters to us. It shows you care."

A simple yet impactful message. Know your presence matters to your people.

FINDING TIME CAN BE HARD

I can relate to the pressures imposed upon you that can make you feel buried.

Like you, I had no shortage of demands on my time. At the corporate office I went from meeting to meeting, always with more things to do. I met with different teams and departments, I was a board member on the provincial association, and I had family concerns, operational situations, and my own mountain of paperwork to attend to. I worked long hours, most weekends, and had a ninety-minute commute at the beginning and end of my day.

I could have allowed all those demands to consume my time and my life. I could have worked endless hours just to get by, only to maintain the current performance of the platform. I would have been busy, but I would have been empty and unfulfilled, and so would my people.

Instead, I chose to prioritize our people, to put our People First. I chose to be with my people every chance I could—in the homes, on the floors, in their meetings, at summits and road shows. I made a choice to conduct road shows at each of our twenty-seven homes twice per year. It was a significant expenditure of my time, but my opportunity to get to know our leaders and team members, to ask them what was working well, acknowledge how they were making a difference, and share my dreams and aspirations for our future. These road shows were a highlight of my career, and it's where I made the greatest difference. Being present with our teams—connecting, sharing, and inspiring—was life-giving and motivational, for them and for me.

Making time enabled me and our people to rise above the daily grind. And we achieved exceptional results. Working together in collaboration, with respect and cohesion, toward our mission and our aspirational goals, we changed lives. We exceeded every goal set for us. We demonstrated what was possible.

Interestingly, our frontline team members got to know me by name and face. They had not had this amount of corporate presence in the past, and it mattered to them. I believe it made them feel that the company cared more about them.

Presence matters. It matters to your team and your customers. Think of a restaurant known for its great food or a store renowned for its high-quality merchandise. That's well and good and goes a long way, but what a difference it makes when the chef takes the time to visit tables and connect with guests, or when a store manager introduces themselves at the end of a sale to express their appreciation for customers' business. Their presence shows they care and leaves a lasting impression.

THE POWER OF NAMES

Calling someone by their name can turn an ordinary, casual conversation into one that's personal and intimate. They become less guarded, more open, and more present. It creates a greater connection, and the opportunity to build a more meaningful relationship presents itself.

We had 240 managers and five thousand team members in our LTC platform. When I was in our homes, I made a concerted effort to call people by their names. It was a demonstration of respect, and I wanted to show them I cared enough to get to know them personally.

I had a couple of techniques I used to recall names. Before going to a home, I would write the managers' names and positions in my notebook and rehearse them. When I met them, I would look them in the eye, shake their hands, and call them by name. They were often surprised. Some would even go so far as to say, "You remembered my name." Evidently it made an impact.

When I was on the floor introducing myself to team members, I would also ask them for the name of the team member just down the hall. When they told me it was "Josephine," I'd walk down the hall and ask Josephine how her day was going. She would be taken aback that I called her by name. I would then ask Josephine the name of the next person. This simple gesture was impactful. It impressed upon the receiver that I cared, that I didn't think of them simply as a number or a position. They were a person first. It's what you'd want for yourself, and it certainly matters to those you lead.

As hard as I tried to get names right, I often failed miserably. But the fact that I tried was acknowledged and appreciated and often ended in me being corrected with a smile and a little laughter.

Captain Michael Abrashoff, in his book *It's Your Ship*, made a point of getting to know all 330 of his sailors. He'd set aside fifteen minutes to meet each one. He would ask them about their family, why they chose to serve, and what they hoped to achieve as a crew member. They would let him know about their family and often said that they wanted "to be somebody" and "make a difference." The captain would then share with them that he wanted the USS *Benfold* to be the best damn ship in the navy, and he invited each sailor to make it their ship.

I'm a great believer in name tags. I use them a lot. I use them because I want to build closer relationships with our people. I try my darnedest to call each person by their name, and name tags serve as a reminder when I forget.

Our corporate office had four hundred people on multiple floors. When I went to get a coffee, I would say hello to those I knew and introduce myself to those I didn't. On one occasion, I asked someone his name and he said, "Mohammad." I asked if he was the person sending me IT requests on behalf of our platform. He said he was. Had I not asked him his name, we would have continued to pass politely in the hallways and lunchroom, never knowing one another. Instead, we made a connection, broke down a barrier, and started to build a more meaningful relationship. This simple act took next to no time and was one small step toward an inclusive, personalized relationship.

APPROACHABILITY

It has been shown that communication is made up of

three components: body language, tone, and spoken words. Surprisingly, body language makes up 55 percent of communication, tone 35 percent, and words only 10 percent. Calling Mohammad by his name, then, was just a small—but important—part of it. Greeting him with a smile and looking him in the eye (body language) and doing it kindly (tone) made up the rest.

If you walk the floors or enter meetings looking for what's good, your body language is going to be open and relaxed. Your tone will be more cheerful and encouraging. But if you're set on identifying what's at fault, what's not working, it's a much different picture. Think of the sound of feet, heavy heels, power postures, perhaps crossed arms. If you were the team member on the floor, who would you like to see come down the hall: an appreciative leader, or someone in command and control? The former one people will gravitate toward; the latter will send them scattering like cockroaches.

What you wear is part of your "body" communication. It too sends a message to your people. Early in my career, I stopped wearing a suit and tie. I looked like a power broker, a hierarchy enforcer. It created a barrier, a distance between myself and my people, and intimidated many. I'm sure I was perceived as "unapproachable."

I intentionally made the change to khakis, a button-down, no tie, and soft-soled dress shoes. It was still professional, without the air of authority. The new outfit, combined with an open and curious demeanor, a mindfulness of the energy I brought to a space, and a desire to look for what was working well, made a real difference. I could tell that these small but significant changes made our people feel more comfortable speaking with me.

I'll contrast this with an example that went too far. I was visiting one of our LTC homes for the first time. The administrator was wearing yoga pants, track shoes, and a loose top. It looked like she had just come from the gym. I could only imagine what a family member would think of this appearance. This outfit did not instill confidence and wasn't reflective of the responsibility held by her position. It was a disappointing first impression.

How we dress communicates a message. It sets an impression. As leaders, we need to do all we can to be at one with our people, all the while representing the professionalism that comes with our position and office.

As for tone: when I sent memos to staff, I didn't refer to my position or title. I would simply state that it was "From: Fraser." I have the good fortune of having an uncommon name, which made this easier, but when I went to homes, summits, or events for IMAGINE—our dementia strategy—I only ever referred to myself by my first name.

I was doing all I could do to make myself as approachable as possible. And it paid off. When attending the IMAGINE sessions I would go from table to table, asking our people about their successes and their greatest takeaways from the teachings. By visiting with them at their tables with their peers, I would often get insights into what was happening at a home, insights I otherwise wouldn't have had.

At one home, I learned of a family member who was constantly berating the team members attending to her mother. They felt bullied, and some would break down in tears. Our leadership had tried to address the family member's behaviour, but their efforts only made matters worse. I brought this matter back to my corporate team, and we gathered specific examples from the home, including the experiences shared with me at the IMAGINE event. We involved our in-house legal counsel and wrote a letter to the family member outlining the need for respect for everyone, by everyone. We let them know that their behaviour was disrespectful of our people and was not welcome.

Fortunately, this intervention was successful. This behaviour would have continued had the team felt uncomfortable speaking with me. At the next training session, they couldn't thank me enough for taking the time to listen to them and act on their behalf.

To be at one with our people, we have to be available to them and they need to know that we welcome their thoughts and observations. Open-door policies have their benefits, but an open door just means you're asking team members to come into your domain, your powerhouse. It can be intimidating. A better way is to be out with your people, in their domain, making yourself available to them. Whether we like it or not, leadership positions come with perceived authority and power. The more we can do to diminish this perception, the better.

Do what you can to make yourself available and approachable to your team. It breaks down barriers, levels the playing field, and creates more opportunities for you and your team to act as one cohesive unit working together toward your greater goals.

CHOOSE THE ENERGY YOU BRING TO A SPACE

You model the way for others to follow. You have the option to choose how you show up. You have to read your current situation and present your best self in the circumstances. I encourage you to exude energy, tone, and body language that are relatable, understandable, and—importantly—predictable.

As for me, I'm emotive. I immerse myself in the feeling of a situation. I'm self-aware and cognizant of the energy I bring to a space. I defer to bring positive, relatable energy. I constantly look for work done well and celebrate accomplishments through stories. Life and business can't always be sunshine and rainbows—challenging situations call for a varied approach. In these situations I'm open, curious, and focused on understanding. When advocating for our residents, people, or homes, I'm predictably more assertive, principled, and strong.

I had an administrator earlier in my career who had extreme, unpredictable highs and lows. His highs were overly enthusiastic and his energy too lofty. He was unrealistic and his team couldn't relate to him. The same happened with his lows: they were exaggerated. He didn't have credibility, and his people didn't know which personality would show up on any given day.

Cecile, another administrator, is a different story. She is a subtle leader. She doesn't say a lot, but when she does speak, she commands a room and your attention. A proud woman, she has high expectations of herself and her team. I used to love touring the floor with Cecile. She called everyone by name, regardless of whether they were team members, residents, or family members. She'd ask about their family or how things were going. On one of the tours, she came across a new staff member she hadn't yet met. She introduced herself, asking the new person her name, where she was from, and a little about her family. Always welcoming, Cecile set the expectation on her first encounter and modelled the way for others to follow.

You get to choose the energy you bring to a space. But know that whenever you're on the floor or in a meeting, all eyes are watching you. You're always on display and you have to present your best self. Your team will be assessing whether you're walking the talk and living up to your own expectations of them.

HOPE AND OPTIMISM

There is always a place for hope and optimism, regardless of your line of work. Workplace challenges abound: markets and the economy take turns for the worse; sales stagnate; customer grievances, personnel shortages, or overtime costs are at all-time highs. Whatever the case, a healthy dose of the glass half-full is always welcome to boost our spirits and encourage us to keep going. In fact, it was never more welcome than when we were living through COVID.

On our video conferences, which were two or three times a week, we would consciously balance new directives and protocols from the Ministry of Health with shout-outs and words of encouragement to those giving it all they had and rising above their pandemic circumstances. We'd acknowledge those who were making progress in containing the virus and celebrate those who were on the other side of an outbreak. We'd share selfies of staff in their personal protective equipment (PPE), residents playing hallway bingo, and even the Toronto Raptors superfan delivering goods and well wishes to our home. We had a wedding held outdoors for our residents to view from inside the home. We played music and danced in our chairs behind our monitors. We shared laughter, and sometimes tears, from emotional overload and exhaustion. We did whatever we could to keep spirits high, all the while being grounded in the reality of our new protocols and the ferocity of the COVID virus.

So please know that there's always a place for hope and optimism, as long as it's grounded in the reality of the day. When you're walking the floors and you're out with your people, know that they will be looking to you to lift their spirits, to instill that sense of hope, to celebrate what's working well, even during challenging times.

LEAVE PEOPLE FEELING BETTER THAN YOU FOUND THEM

Whether I was meeting people in their offices or homes or on road shows, I frequently got the feedback that they felt uplifted or energized, that I had given them the boost they needed. The general ethos of my engagements was positivity.

As you've learned, operating in LTC can be arduous. Sometimes we had to work through challenges. I would listen intently and, without judgment, respond gently with suggestions. So whether I was simply providing support, giving a boost of encouragement, or providing more confidence to overcome hurdles, people felt inspired to do more and better equipped to tackle the challenges at hand.

On one occasion, when I was walking the floors of one of our homes and introducing myself to team members, I came across Gail, a housekeeper, so I introduced myself. She didn't hear me well and asked for my name again. I said I was Fraser, the vice president of LTC operations.

"Oh, you don't want to talk to me," she said.

"I do," I confirmed.

"You don't have enough time to hear what I have to say."

"I'll take the time," I said.

We stood there for twenty minutes. She ran through a number of observations and items that her department could use to be more effective, and I listened intently and paraphrased her concerns so she knew I understood them. By the end of the conversation, she had become visually more relaxed and her body language had softened.

She thanked me for taking the time to listen. I could tell that she knew I had given her my full attention and that she was surprised that "someone in my position" would take the time with her. She felt heard and seen. And we acted on and implemented her recommendations.

On another occasion I had the opportunity to present to a different group, thanks to Linda, someone I worked closely with. Linda was my business partner responsible for LTC finance. She was on a committee creating an education day for the finance, IT, and decision-support departments and invited me to speak. They had a full agenda and an early start at 8:00 a.m. I was the first speaker for the day.

With the room still waking with the help of coffee, I started playing "Ain't No Mountain High Enough," sung by Michael McDonald. I began dancing and singing the chorus and invited the half-asleep group to join me. It took a while. Some joined in; many smiled at my singing or dancing or both. By the end of the song, spirits had lifted, people were animated, and I had their attention.

I spoke about the importance of a vision and working toward it, the strength and beauty to be found in the interdependence of teamwork, and how our greatest opportunities are realized when we're working in collaboration with others. I outlined the operational circumstances that we encountered in LTC and how we were rising above them. And I finished by encouraging them to live into their potential and strive to be all they could be.

I gave them a jolt of energy and thoughtfulness that was stronger than the caffeine in their cups. I left them feeling better than I found them. Later, Linda would often tell me about the impact I had that day. She was never more proud of what we were doing in the LTC platform and how we were leading the way.

When you devote time to harnessing the energy you bring to a space, you leave a lasting impression wherever you go. Lift people up, and you'll leave them wanting to do more, to be more, to live into their potential.

TAKE THE TIME TO RESET AND CENTRE

I mentioned earlier that you need to present your best self. But let's be honest: you're not always going to be in the lightest of moods. After finishing a difficult call, conducting a challenging meeting, receiving news of yet another regulatory change, or any number of other issues you as a leader have to contend with, you know your mind will not always be in the right place to go to the floor. You simply won't be your best self, nor will you be able to model the presence you want others to replicate. That's not the way you want to show up.

These circumstances will happen. And when they do, be good to yourself and your team by taking the time to reset and centre your mood and your energy. Take a deep breath or a short walk. Do what works for you to get back to a place where you feel composed and can show up fully, so that when you go to the floor, you're the best version of yourself, the one you want others to see. As always, be the example.

Sometimes these energy shifts can come suddenly. You could be on the floor and a customer or one of your team members confronts you in front of others. If you feel your ire building and sense that things are going the wrong way, respectfully ask that you continue the discussion in your office, or some other private place, at a mutually agreeable time. This will give you a chance to compose yourself and to prepare for the meeting with an open and curious mindset, without the pressure of an audience.

For example, one of our administrators was talented, passionate, considerate, dedicated, and loving—an incredible advocate for her residents—but she had a shortcoming. She would allow some individuals to get under her skin, to push her buttons to the point where her emotions got the better of her. She would react abruptly, leave meetings or the building. This response weakened her credibility and predictability as a leader. We worked with her to strengthen her resolve and encouraged her to reset and centre in those moments when she was feeling compromised.

There's a saying often attributed to Viktor Frankl, from *Man's Search for Meaning*, that goes something like this: "Between stimulus and response lies the power to choose." When you're confronted, remember that you can choose how to respond. Remember, too, that you can't take back the things you might say or do in the heat of the moment.

Better to temper your thoughts and comments and save them for the appropriate time. You, and the others, will be glad you did.

CHAPTER 4
Higher Purpose

Setting a higher purpose is the starting point to living a bigger life.

We all have an innate desire to do more and be more. We need to know that our lives are worthwhile and that we make a difference.

We've all set personal goals at one time or another: getting fit, finding a better job, making a team, being a better parent. It's when we're working toward these goals that we feel more alive. More alive because we're striving for something bigger, something better.

And that's no different for our people. They too have a desire to live into a higher purpose. They need to know that their life is worthwhile, that they make a difference.

Setting and sharing a higher purpose, with passion and enthusiasm, is not only key to living a bigger life personally—it's also an essential step to overcoming the disengagement epidemic, one that moves you toward your greater goal, the future state that you and your people want and need.

In *The Innovation Secrets of Steve Jobs,* Carmine Gallo writes, "Every innovation at Apple starts with a big, bold vision, and healthy dose of inspiration." Bianca Andreescu, a Canadian tennis player, uses meditation and visualization to create a winning mindset. She pictures herself playing her best game, using her best techniques, and winning the day. Arnold Schwarzenegger came to the US at the age of sixteen with a strong, clear, compelling vision: to become a movie star.

In each of these examples, their vision constantly reminds them of the higher purpose they intended to realize. They kept it front and centre, top of mind, consciously in focus, and persistently worked toward it. The result: Apple is one of the most successful tech companies in the world, Bianca is a Canadian tennis champion, and Arnold is a film legend.

Strong visions open up a new world of possibilities for you and your team. The impact can be life-changing. The greater the excitement and enthusiasm you generate, the more progress you'll make toward your goal and the higher the probability you'll achieve your future state.

BRING YOUR MISSION TO LIFE

Most organizations have a mission, a vision, and values that hang on their walls, are posted on their website, or live in their manuals. Most are lengthy and all-encompassing. Many aren't easily remembered or recited. Even when brief and memorable, they remain lifeless, are seldom referred to, and don't play an active role in day-to-day operations.

To be effective, to be of use, the mission, vision, and values have to live in the hearts and minds of the people. They need to be referred to often, made part of team discussions, and celebrated with accomplishments and initiatives that align with them.

When I was applying to Chartwell, I took it upon myself to learn and memorize their mission, vision, and values before my interview. Their mission is "to provide a happier, healthier, and more fulfilling life experience for seniors." Their vision is "to make people's lives better." And their values were based on the acronym RESPECT: respect, empathy, service excellence, performance, education, commitment, and trust.

I had previously worked with the organization's senior executives and held them in high regard. As I went through the interview process, I referenced their mission, vision, and values. I took the opportunity to align them with my personal motto of Making Others More. I explained that by prioritizing and focusing on the needs of our people, enabling them to live into their potential, and aligning their efforts to a higher purpose, any organization could prosper.

During onboarding, other new hires and I learned how to access our computers and received a basic overview of software, significant policies, benefits, and the company's mission, vision, and values. I was struck by how quickly and nonchalantly the latter were covered. It felt obligatory, lacking depth, heart, or meaning. In short, lifeless.

Over the next few months I observed the culture of the company generally, and of my team and homes specifically. The vision—"making people's lives better"—was well known and constantly referred to. The mission was rarely referred to and little known. Our LTC homes were well run, comprehensive policies and practices were in place, and my leadership team had talent and experience, as did the teams leading most of the homes. Their focus was intentionally corporate. They were driven by financial performance and compliance with Ministry of Health standards and inspection outcomes. Annually there was significant focus given to resident satisfaction and employee engagement surveys.

As I stated in the introduction, operating in long-term

care is rigorous and can be arduous. It can be hard at times to see beyond the daily demands. Having been in the sector for twenty-five years, I understood the never-ending internal and external demands and challenges our leaders faced. I could tell our people were tired and at times overwhelmed.

But I also knew those leading and serving in LTC were passionate, compassionate, and driven to make a difference in the lives of others. I knew from experience that they longed for the opportunity to bring their passion to life. They needed to reconnect their passion with their work. They needed a lift, some inspiration, a higher purpose that they could really live into.

Formally proposing a change to Chartwell's mission, vision, and values would have taken a lot of time, and frankly the senior executives were committed to them as they were.

So we did the next best thing. We revitalized and prioritized the current mission and gave it new life. It was "To provide a happier, healthier, more fulfilling life experience for seniors." For me it was aspirational. This was an ideal goal to strive for.

Breaking it down made our desired impact even more clear: our higher purpose was to provide "happier," "healthier," "more fulfilling life experiences" for our residents. It was beautiful. I mean, who doesn't want that in their life? I certainly do. And why not make it our focus for residents and our people alike?

ASPIRATIONAL GOALS

Once we revitalized the mission, we set out to create specific and aspirational goals that would help support it. We took our cue from the UVP, or unique value proposition: "delivering WOW." We asked ourselves: What initiatives might we take to deliver WOW for our residents? What initiatives would make them happier, what might they be doing to be healthier, and how could we make their experiences more fulfilling? It was perfect. If we successfully implemented and practiced it, we could deliver on our mission.

To make it more tangible, more relatable, we narrowed the WOW factor into four distinct areas of focus that tied into our satisfaction surveys: they were the Dining Experience, Social/Recreational Initiatives, Dementia Care, and Palliative Care. We would call these our "4 Pillars of WOW."

We presented the revitalized mission and 4 Pillars of WOW to our platform of 240 leaders for their consideration and approval.

They were excited and energized about the new focus and the possibilities that the future held. It reignited their passion, and I witnessed a hunger for the possibilities that transcended compliance. Clearly, they too wanted their lives to stand for something more than merely compliance. They wanted to do more of the work they loved. It was a magical feeling for everyone. They hadn't felt this invigorated in years. The energy in the room was palpable, and we hadn't even got started yet. They were all in.

When you share your higher purpose and aspirational goals with passion and enthusiasm, your leaders and team members will follow along and envision what the future can be. Without even getting started, you'll create excitement and possibilities in the minds of your people.

CREATE A MOTTO FOR YOUR MOVEMENT

In addition to the mission and 4 Pillars, we introduced the concept of Rising Above the Regs, which we often abbreviated to Rising Above. We felt it captured our desire and drive to do more, and be more, than the regulations. It became our motto, our call to disrupt business as usual, do things differently, and demonstrate what was possible. It was aspirational, actionable, and easily remembered and stated. It incorporated our vision and mission and our 4 Pillars of WOW. Combined, the motto would propel our people and platform to new heights. We would no longer play small and simply comply with the regulations. We would Rise Above them.

Our motto served, too, as a consistent reminder that we were destined to be more. It was ever present. It lived in our hearts and minds. It permeated our conversations, discussions, team meetings, road shows, leadership summits, and conferences.

Achievable

And it resonated throughout the organization. Other divisions and the corporate office watched on as we in long-term care—often considered an underdog, an afterthought—would rise up and achieve unprecedented outcomes. We became the platform leading change in the organization. We were Rising Above our regulatory circumstances, improving compliance, exceeding our financial goals, and making exceptional gains on our satisfaction survey results. We became synonymous with Rising Above.

KEEP YOUR HIGHER PURPOSE TOP OF MIND

Our administrators completed a monthly report that summarized financial performance, operational priorities, ministry compliance, labour relations, and workers' compensation. It was comprehensive. It was also cumbersome.

Each year we were given the opportunity to fine-tune the document. Together with my directors, we consolidated the report, removed redundancies for information collected elsewhere, and, importantly, incorporated the 4 Pillars of WOW. This addition emphasized our expectation that the leaders at each home take initiatives that would enable them to work toward our higher purpose. Providing "happier, healthier, more fulfilling life experiences" for our residents was once again front and centre.

SETTING EXPECTATIONS

With a constant eye on our mission and vision, 4 Pillars, and motto, we set high standards and high expectations for our people, and they embraced them with pride and accomplishment. So much so that within two years our "very satisfied" score for residents increased by 15 percent, when our corporate target was to achieve an increase of 2 percent. Our platform blew expectations out of the water. In fact, our five-year stretch goal was to reach a "very satisfied" result of 57 percent, and in two years we were at 58 percent. We had already exceeded our five-year target.

I asked our administrators what our new target should be, considering we'd already beaten the previous one in two years.

Before I reveal their answer, let me give some context. When the senior executive set the goals for the platforms in the past, long-term care was given some leniency. It was understood that it was far harder to achieve the same levels of resident satisfaction in LTC than in retirement living. LTC's resident needs were higher and more complex, and almost 100 percent of its homes were unionized. We had almost three times as many team members per resident, the ministry inspected our homes on a regular basis, and family members had higher expectations given the complexity of their loved ones' care. Indeed, it was understandably harder to achieve the same levels of satisfaction in LTC.

However, with these results, we were making headway and catching up to our peers in the retirement platform. Their five-year goal was a "very satisfied" score of 67 percent. So, what did our administrators think our new goal in LTC should be?

"Sixty-eight percent!"

Yes, that's right. They now believed in themselves so much that they were prepared to set our target 1 percent higher than their retirement peers.

To paraphrase author Carmine Gallo, "If a leader communicates a compelling vision and holds their teams to high expectations, their teams will respond to meet them. They will work harder, dream bigger, and find ways to make the impossible possible." And that's exactly what our team did. No one ever expected LTC could match the satisfaction levels of the retirement platform, and here we were setting our sights even higher. We were prepared to make the impossible possible.

Whether you're leading a company or a department within one, establish a higher purpose for yourself and those you lead. Don't limit your ideas. Whether you create a new mission or bring the existing one back to life, do it with passion, energy, and enthusiasm and invite your people to join you on the journey.

Just like Apple, Bianca, and Arnold, you too can

achieve your goals with a strong, compelling vision that's top of mind and always in focus that you work toward every day.

CHAPTER 5

The 3 E's of People First Leadership

You need not look any further than within the walls of your company to find greatness.

Changing the way you lead is the next step in the progressive sequence, the next concentric circle.

I've distilled the People First leadership principles into three key words: *engage*, *enable*, and *empower*. It's simple, yet robust and comprehensive. If we genuinely believe that people are the means to the success of any business, our responsibility as leaders is to create an environment that *engages* our people in a better, brighter future, *enables* them by investing in their skills and talents, and *empowers* them to act in the best interest of the business and its customers.

ENGAGE

To engage your people is to inspire and persuade them to adapt to new ways, not impose it upon them.

We've covered focusing on work done well, being cognizant of how you show up, and creating a higher purpose and aspirational goals. These are the stepping stones of engagement. You've started the wheels turning in the minds of your people. They're intrigued. They're starting to get excited. You're well on your way to moving the needle on the disengagement epidemic.

The key to building momentum with your people is to engage them. It's the ability to pique their curiosity, entice them to do things differently, or inspire them to rise to the occasion. To explain the reason for a change in direction, answer the question "What's in it for me (WIFM)?" and paint a picture of how it will make their lives better.

Sure, you can command your people to change their ways instead. That may get you quicker results. It may even work a few times. But with each demand you'll build resentment. The more you impose your will, the more disengaged they'll become. They'll start to check out because neither they nor their thoughts and opinions are being appreciated.

Like you, your people want to understand the reason for change, new directions, or new policies. They'll be willing to follow you if you help them understand the importance of change, the difference it would make, and how it will make your service better. Once the new initiative is implemented, you'll want to touch base with your team to see how it's going, what's working well, and what outcomes they're achieving. Solicit success stories, ask for their thoughts, and provide more clarity, resources, and skills when needed. The more time you invest up front engaging your people, the more buy-in and momentum you'll create over time.

I was no longer willing to do management training the same old way. We weren't going to hold management "retreats" where we would introduce new policies and procedures and give our people more things to do. No, we weren't going to do that. We would have intentional Leadership Summits. These would be "live into your potential" summits. Summits where we would engage our people in a better, brighter future.

These summits were my launching pad, my opportunity to engage and entice our people in a new direction and bring our revitalized mission back to life. It was at one such summit, in fact, that I first introduced Rising Above the Regs and the 4 Pillars of WOW.

Achievable

The energy and enthusiasm coming out of these sessions was incredible. Our people really needed this change in perspective. It was a way to get beyond the daily grind, to be with their people and do more of the work they loved. They were engaged and excited about our future together.

ENABLE

To enable your people is to provide them with the skills, knowledge, and resources to grow, to be better, and to make a greater impact.

As we know from articulating a higher purpose, we feel most alive when we're working toward something bigger, something better. Whether you're providing training, leading a sales session, or mentoring, you're giving people tools and techniques to grow, to make a greater contribution, and to create a more meaningful impact. And by investing in their knowledge, you'll be increasing retention too—team members are far more likely to stay when they feel valued and appreciated.

I defer to being inclusive of and transparent with others, as opposed to exclusive and guarded with knowledge and information. I believe being inclusive enables your people to be greater contributors to your community.

We had regular platform meetings with our directors

and consultants. The consultants were our "subject-matter experts" in nursing, nutritional care, program and support services, and environmental services. To broaden the depth and scope of support to our homes, I extended an open invitation to our HR managers, project managers, and accounting team to join the platform meetings. Although they formally reported to other departments, they were dedicated to supporting our LTC homes. I wanted them to feel a sense of belonging and connectedness with our strategies and to understand the extent of our education and initiatives.

For me, the HR team was integral to the success of the LTC platform. They met frequently with our homes, people, and unions and became very familiar with our People First initiatives. They participated in platform meetings, leadership summits, road shows, and IMAGINE—our dementia training. We enabled them with the same skills, knowledge, and resources we were sharing with our people. I wanted them to experience the lengths to which we were going to change lives—for both our residents and our team—and in turn share that knowledge with our unions so that they too had a sense of how we were doing things differently.

EMPOWER

To empower your people is to unleash their passion, talent, and resolve to create and implement new initiatives.

Achievable

Trust is at the base of all empowerment. Trust is earned when you, as leader, let go and demonstrate your belief in your people. It's a show of support and an encouragement to try. Today's teams don't become tomorrow's leaders without it.

A simple and beautiful way to empower someone is to personally invite them to lead a project. The act of letting them know that you've identified them, among their peers, as having the strength, courage, and competence to lead is one of the greatest compliments you can extend to someone.

At one of our homes we had a notable COVID outbreak. We were working with and accountable to the local health authority for making progress. Our leadership team was on-site around the clock. They were conducting audits on every shift and in every resident neighbourhood. They were conducting and compiling up to two hundred audits per day.

Yet, despite those efforts, the new variant of the virus remained persistent.

Not to be outdone, the administrator came up with an incredible idea. She proposed that they invite a personal support worker (PSW) from each shift, in each neighbourhood, to coach and mentor their peers on proper techniques for putting on and taking off PPE, hand hygiene, and environmental cleaning.

She identified PSWs on each shift and in each

neighbourhood who had the respect of their peers. She approached each one personally and invited them to be the PSW IPAC (infection prevention and control) lead for their shift. Honoured to be asked, they committed to doing everything necessary to help fight the outbreak. Each PSW—empowered to lead—rose to the challenge, helped their peers, conducted audits, and was integral in helping the home see the other side of the outbreak.

This is a story I've told many times. I was so proud of that team and the administrator's insight to do things differently—to recognize the talent in her people and to empower those individuals to play a key role in getting the virus under control. It was a long haul. They were exhausted by the end of it, but so very proud of what they had done together to win the day.

EMBRACE THE INSIGHTS OF YOUR PEOPLE

Avril was a food and nutrition manager at one of our older homes. It had one hundred residents and one dining room for everyone. She applied for a position at one of our new homes with 187 residents, eight floors, and eight dining rooms. At this home they consistently received mediocre results from the resident satisfaction survey for dining room service. They struggled to coordinate meal service across multiple floors at the same time.

Avril was a young but wise leader. She came into the new position without ego. She let the team know that her previous home had only one dining room—much easier to coordinate meal service—and she acknowledged that the team at her new home had worked there for years, and that they would know best about how to improve the service.

Avril met with residents and asked about their meals, the service, and the quality of the dining experience. She shared the residents' feedback with her team, worked beside them to understand their challenges, and invited them to share their ideas to make the service better. She involved her team in menu planning, identified those meals that were time intensive, looked for ready-made alternatives, and created an advanced production schedule with tasks shared among team members based on their input.

Together they put those ideas into action. Avril was an inclusive and collaborative leader who empowered her team to work as one and improve the dining experience.

THE AGENCY HUB

During the pandemic our staffing resources were stretched. Like most operators in LTC, when we were in outbreak, staffing levels were more challenging because many team members would become symptomatic or test positive for COVID. This was a time when we needed additional resources, not fewer.

Our residents often were confined to and received meals in their rooms, and team members had to take more time to don and doff their PPE between each resident. The leadership teams in the homes had to focus on containing the outbreak and ensuring our protocols were in place and practiced. But, too often, they were spending a significant portion of their day finding additional staff, working with staffing agencies to fulfil a staffing ratio of at least 1.5 times our normal daily quota. Their attention needed to be on the outbreak, not staffing.

We had different homes in outbreak contacting the same agencies. We were adding agencies to our roster almost daily. It became chaotic. We were competing with ourselves, as well as other health-care providers, for limited resources.

Our HR team was also working tirelessly, at all hours of the day, to find staff to resource our homes. We began to frustrate the agencies with multiple requests for the same home.

Knowing we needed to streamline the agency process, our HR team came up with the concept of the Agency Hub. The idea was to centralize the coordination of agency staff for the homes. They invited Tammy, a talented, composed, and optimistic HR specialist, to lead the Hub. She would work with our HR team to identify the needs of the homes, and the Hub would assign agency staff to them.

This was empowerment in action, and a perfect

example of "finding a way to say yes." Our HR team identified a need and developed a solution. All I had to do was say yes and set them free to put it into action. Did I trust them? Absolutely! Was it perfect at first? No. Was it messy? Yes. Did the team have the wherewithal and flexibility to figure it out? Without a doubt. And they did. Did I interfere? No. I was fully confident they would succeed. It was so successful, in fact, that the company used a hybrid of the same model to support the retirement side of the business.

• • •

Let me lay out two other examples that pull together the 3 *E*'s of People First leadership.

SEE THE STRENGTH IN OTHERS

A mark of a great leader is the ability to notice the strength in others who don't see it in themselves. It could be that team members want to work on the same shift as these individuals because they bring good energy; have a gentle, collaborative spirit; or simply know how to liven things up, rally their coworkers, and have fun. Or they could be the ones who take charge when something goes wrong, or who are quick to support their peers when they need a hand.

Generally, these individuals would say they're just doing their job; they don't see what they're doing as special.

Our responsibility as leaders is to look for these individuals and find or create opportunities for them to shine.

Shawn is one such individual. She started her career at OMNI as a nurse's aide at the age of sixteen, at Springdale, a small home outside Peterborough, Ontario. This was in the days before health-care aides and personal support workers. It wasn't long before she was recognized by her peers and elected as their union steward. She had great rapport, an incredible sense of humour, and a strong work ethic, and she could be counted on to lend a hand when needed. A short time thereafter she was elected chief steward for her home.

Given Shawn's affinity with her teammates and how effectively she worked with the home's management, she easily secured the position of office manager in one of our neighbouring homes. Although this was a very different role, she demonstrated that she was up to the challenge.

We had identified Shawn as someone capable of more and encouraged her to apply for the role of office manager at the corporate office. Throughout my career, I've come to know many union representatives and stewards like Shawn, and I've seen a great number of them become incredible managers and leaders.

Although apprehensive about taking on the new role and leaving the safety and familiarity of the homes, she came on board. We were confident that she would adapt. And she did. And did it well.

Achievable

She would grow into that role and excelled in every position she assumed. We saw her potential and knew she could master every opportunity she was given, even when she didn't believe she could. She joined our operations team and became a certified Supportive Measures specialist (a dementia specialist). She learned more about medications and antipsychotics than most of our registered staff. And she became renowned as the most respected "non-nurse" in the sector. Today, Shawn is the chief operating officer at OMNI. We engaged, enabled, and empowered Shawn to live into her potential. She got there on her own merit. She is admired and respected by her people and sets the example for others to follow.

IMAGINE . . . LIVING LIFE TO YOUR POTENTIAL

IMAGINE . . . Living Life to Your Potential, our dementia strategy, was our single greatest accomplishment at Chartwell, in my view. IMAGINE is the culmination of many of this book's teachings and exemplifies what's possible when you engage, enable, and empower your people.

Remember, dementia care was one of our 4 Pillars of WOW. We wanted to be one of the premier dementia-care providers in the province.

First, we identified and invited leaders who had a strong interest in dementia and were influencers within our LTC platform. Carey, our program consultant, was well versed in Montessori practices. Lisa was a registered nurse and administrator and director of care at one of our homes. Deb was a director of regional operations and a creator and teacher of Living Tapestry, a holistic and comprehensive approach to resident care. Each was honoured and delighted to be invited to the project. I was part of it too. I had helped commission our dementia strategy at OMNI.

Initially we discussed our hopes and aspirations for our strategy. We wanted our program to be all-encompassing, highlighting the different dementias, how the disease presents itself, and how our team members could best support those living with it.

We explored many strong dementia-care offerings that already existed. The Ontario-based Research Institute for Aging's LIVING the Dementia Journey is relationship based and focused on understanding each individual—their history, occupations, likes, and dislikes. Dementia-care specialist Teepa Snow's Positive Approach to Care, a newer program, was getting lots of attention. Teepa specializes in how to approach residents to best support them. DementiAbility, a dementia program spearheaded by gerontologist Gail Elliot, is based on Montessori theories, engaging residents in the daily activities of life. We also looked at GPA, or Gentle Persuasive Approaches, a teaching based on its namesake—gentle approaches—and being used in many of our homes. We referenced the dementia program I had experienced at OMNI, authored by Len Fabiano and called Supportive Measures.

While each of these programs was good in its own right, none of them was the comprehensive offering we were looking for.

So we went back to the drawing board. We didn't want to confine ourselves to traditional norms or established programs. As we have expressed throughout this book, we put our People First. We dreamt about what our dementia strategy could be, what would best empower our frontline team members, and how our approach would enable our residents to lead happier, healthier, more fulfilling lives.

We embarked on the journey to create our own dementia strategy, one that would incorporate—with permission—some of the teachings of other programs. Each of us was empowered to develop a section of the program. Lisa would become our IMAGINE leader to champion and develop the curriculum around the attributes and characteristics of dementia. She became certified in the Positive Approach to Care. Carey participated in LIVING the Dementia Journey, and we incorporated many of the teachings of DementiAbility too. Deb helped Carey develop the social-recreational component of the program. I developed the leadership training, as we would be relying on the participants to go back to their homes, share their teachings, and lead by example on the floor.

And we went further. We brought in Deborah Bakti, a former LTC executive married to an LTC resident. She wrote *Recipe for Empathy: Six Strategies to Transform Your Families into Fans in Seniors' Care*, to help LTC team members look through the eyes of families and empathize with their experiences. Her insights were of great value to our people who every day supported passionate, and at times difficult to work with, families.

We introduced IMAGINE to our platform meeting at our national convention in early 2019, and the inaugural program launched that March.

We identified and invited team members who we knew were enthusiastic about the program and could rally their peers. We were building a community of IMAGINE influencers. We wanted and needed to build a base of supporters for future training.

We intentionally did not invite resistors, or those who "needed" the training, to these initial sessions. We knew we would have to address them with time and were confident that they would become willing participants once they saw that the teachings achieved better outcomes.

We held four regional education sessions to minimize travel for our team members. We would train off-site for four days, one full day every month for four months. At the end of each session, we would give the participants a workplace project so they could apply what they had learned. At the beginning of the next, we would ask them to tell us about their projects and experiences. We called this Applied Learning.

The energy in these sessions was incredible. It was experiential and tactile and included role-playing. We laughed and learned together. We incorporated inspirational videos. We referenced great authors like Brené Brown, Maya Angelou, and Michael Abrashoff.

We *engaged* our participants by helping them envision new and better ways for our residents to live more fulfilling lives. We *enabled* them with new skills and knowledge, and *empowered* them to adapt the new practices to meet the needs of individual residents. We enlivened their spirits with hope, purpose, and belonging. We were creating a culture of possibility and potential, for everyone.

Just before the pandemic hit, we had graduated 750 IMAGINE ambassadors. At the end of the program we presented them with IMAGINE shirts, a badge of honour they would wear with pride in their homes.

It was such a shame to have to stop the IMAGINE training sessions to focus on COVID-19. We had created such incredible momentum. I can only imagine how high we would have gone had the course been able to continue.

I can say with confidence that IMAGINE was the

single greatest game changer in my career. It was created and led by our best and brightest. It brought light and life into the hearts of our people. It changed the way they saw their jobs. It honoured and empowered them to grow into their potential. It was life-changing for those who participated and life-giving for our residents.

Today it gives me great pleasure knowing that Lisa, Carey, Deb, and Deborah are once again leading the IMAGINE sessions.

EXTREME OWNERSHIP

In *Extreme Ownership: How US Navy Seals Lead and Win,* author Jocko Willink writes of the importance of leadership and self-reflection. He believes that leaders should take full responsibility for the outcomes of their teams. If they're not achieving the outcomes they hope for, a leader should reflect on their own actions and ask themselves what they could have done differently: Were they clear in their direction? Did they believe it was understood? Did they invite team members to ask for clarity? Was their tone and body language open to feedback or input, or were they perceived as closed and definitive? Did their team have the resources they needed? Did they have the equipment and skill needed to do what the leader was asking? Was there something they overlooked, or were there challenges that could have been predicted and circumvented?

In other words, no matter how much you engage, enable, and empower your team, being a People First leader means that at the end of the day, the outcomes—good or bad—fall to you.

Taking ownership is important and impactful. It avoids the "blame game," finger-pointing to absolve oneself of responsibility, which perpetuates a culture of distrust. Instead, it sets a high standard and high expectation for yourself and a great example for others to follow.

When you've reflected on an undesirable outcome and determined which remedial actions you personally need to take, debrief with your team and let them know your thoughts on how and what you, as their leader, need to change to achieve a better outcome.

Once you've disclosed what you believe you can do better, ask them what they think went wrong and how to improve it. What you'll find—especially with time and trust—is that when you expose your own vulnerabilities and humbly identify where you need to improve, your team will follow suit. They too will identify what they could do better. Collectively, upon reflection, you'll be setting up yourself and your team for a more successful future.

As a leader I spent a lot of time in self-reflection, especially when driving back from a home visit or a corporate or association meeting. I would ask myself what went well and what I could have done better. I would ask myself if I brought good energy to a space. Was I open and approachable? Could I have said or positioned things differently so that they were better understood or created greater buy-in? I would be hard on myself if I felt meetings, and my part in them, could have been better.

When I was in the homes, I tended to be my best self. I knew my role: focus on what was working well, bring out the best in people, and lift spirits. I found new stories and shared stories from other homes. I would say the same was true when we had platform meetings or summits with our administrators and managers. I felt I brought good energy to corporate meetings, and I was always willing to participate and challenge strategies when I thought they could be better or if they didn't go far enough to support our people or platform.

I would say that as a board member of our association, I could come across as strong minded and strong willed to a fault. I've always been an advocate for the greater good of our residents, staff, owners, and the sector. Because of my passion, coupled with my integrity and desire to do what's right and not what's easy, I could push hard on issues, where others would let them go. I've never regretted my stance on principled issues. On reflection though, I could have tempered my tone and persistence and still achieved similar outcomes. Lessons learned.

CHAPTER 6

People-Focused Communication

Whether you lead a nation, an enterprise, a community, or a family, we are all in the communication business.

—Robin Sharma

In your career, have you ever wondered what was going on at your company? Felt like you were being intentionally left out? Heard the rumour mill gaining volume? Or maybe you were given tasks or informed of policy changes but never the reasons why? My guess is that you have, many times.

Achievable

In a similar vein, do you think your team ever feels the same way? Are there some people or departments that are better informed than others? It's not ideal, but it's all too common in organizations that don't put People First.

I've spent years watching corporate offices send new policies, procedures, and directives to their operating divisions, convinced that it counted as good communication. It's not. That's not communication. It's just more things to do. Heck, earlier in my career I watched it happen in my own company. Leadership, operations, and HR pumping out never-ending to-dos, changing procedures for reasons unknown to most team members. These were directives, orders, one-way communications without the opportunity for feedback.

Communication is integral to the success of any business. It's the next step in the progressive sequence to create a culture of possibility and potential. It's the conduit that keeps your team informed, motivated, and engaged. It weaves its way through updates, changes, stories, and new initiatives. It should be ever present.

Effective communication creates transparency, trust, inclusion, cohesion, and understanding.

People-focused communication puts People First. It considers what they need to know, want to know, and like to know. It is comprehensive and timely. It provides situational awareness and celebrates accomplishments and gives shout-outs to colleagues and departments making progress aligned with aspirational goals. It's inclusive of everyone and all departments.

If you want to change your culture, change what you communicate.

Let's face it, we all want to feel important enough to be informed and have the opportunity to ask questions, seek clarity, and understand where we're going and why. That's how we adapt more readily to change.

So let's not limit communication to new directives. There's a lot going on throughout our days. There are people doing incredible work—other departments, and the individuals within them working on projects. There are events that require coordination, and stories of individuals and teams rising above and knocking it out of the park. There are also challenges and conflicts that need to be addressed.

Consider how you might feel if you were a team member experiencing this brand of communication, both for the first time and consistently thereafter. I bet you'd feel more informed and included, more respected and appreciated. Your sense of pride and belonging would be stronger. You'd be a more willing team member. You'd want to make a greater contribution. Synergies among teams would improve, and barriers between departments would break down.

Achievable

And that rumour mill? Effective people-focused communication squashes it. Informed people aren't operating in a "cone of silence"; they'll make fewer assumptions, fill in less blanks, and engage in little gossip. They will be well informed and won't have to.

TEAM UPS

COVID-19 presented the most challenging of times for the LTC sector, especially as we tended to society's most vulnerable population. In the early days, little was known about the virus, how it would hide in victims for days before showing its symptoms, all the while infecting those providing and receiving care. PPE supply was compromised, and PCR, or rapid testing, didn't yet exist. Our people didn't want to spread the virus, let alone bring it home to their unsuspecting families. They were understandably scared. They didn't know what they didn't know. These days were chaotic, unpredictable, and merciless.

Never was there a more important time to keep all our people informed.

Prior to COVID, we had been working on our daily communications, which we call Team Ups. It was similar to the "lineups" practiced and taught by Ritz-Carlton.

As I mentioned early in this book, Team Ups were fifteen-to-twenty-minute standing meetings. We held them in every resident neighbourhood within the home, on all three shifts with all team members from all departments serving those neighbourhoods, not just nursing. Our leaders, if not on-site, would alternate who held a Zoom call at 11:00 p.m. to share and discuss information with the night staff.

Our people never felt more informed and included.

We shared new information and protocols from the Ministry of Health. We reviewed audit results and gave updates on how many residents had tested positive for COVID, how many cases had resolved, and who had succumbed to it. We did the same for the number of team members who'd tested positive and were symptomatic. We had different team members model how to don and doff PPE, and others demonstrate how to clean surfaces or effectively sanitize hands. We used a black light to highlight good cleaning practices. And we shared successes and stories of our people and departments going the extra mile.

Team Ups were two-way communication. These were times of real fear and apprehension. Our team members would ask about the safety of the PPE and whether two face masks were better than one. They would express their anxiety, individually and collectively. And while our leaders did their best to give assurances, they could not give guarantees. Too much was unknown about the virus. At these Team Ups our people rallied one another, they consoled each other, they dug in and found strength in one another to keep going.

Achievable

These were meetings that nobody wanted to miss. They were informative, inclusive, and supportive. There was a spirit of collaboration, one of all hands on deck, of everyone doing what they could to help one another, regardless of department.

The pandemic taught us much, sometimes the hard way, but one of its silver linings was Team Ups. They represented the very best of people-focused communication. Transparent and honest, they built trust within our teams. Inclusive, they fostered unprecedented cohesion, teamwork, understanding, and appreciation. They were the glue that held our people together through precarious times. They helped our people overcome the virus.

Regardless of your industry or circumstances, Team Ups can be an effective people-focused communication strategy for you and your team.

SHARING YOUR ADVOCACY EFFORTS

Like you, I've had occasion to advocate for my people. For me that meant seeking salary increases on behalf of my team, opposing provincial directives, or objecting to ministry findings. Most often we as leaders work away at these advocacy efforts in the background, without our people knowing the lengths to which we go on their behalf.

In *It's Your Ship*, Michael Abrashoff, a former US

Navy captain, writes of a time he challenged the admiral's orders. Against navy protocol, he broadcast the conversation over the loudspeakers so that the sailors could hear him. It was a heated discussion. In the end, Michael didn't win his argument, but he did demonstrate to his sailors that he went to bat for them. He had gained their respect and established that he had their backs. I'm not suggesting you put your conversations on loudspeaker (nor is Michael). But I encourage you to let your people know when you advocate on their behalf.

In the case of salary increases, I've often communicated many of my advocacy efforts to smaller leadership groups. And in administrator meetings I've discussed my efforts to increase staffing or lobby for new funding from the provincial government, or expressed my opposition to clinical-documentation tools that would have added to the workload of our registered staff.

During my time at OMNI, the government at the time proposed a regulation that required every Ontario LTC home have registered nurses (RNs) on-site twenty-four hours a day, seven days a week. Ordinarily, smaller, rural homes had registered practical nurses (RPNs) work evening and night shifts, with an RN on call. This new proposal had significant ramifications. For one, it meant we would have to let go our RPNs who worked evenings and nights. This frustrated me.

To be clear, I hold RNs in high regard and honour the work they do. But our RPNs—most of them long tenured—had for years built rapport with our residents. They were loyal and predictable. RNs, who were in high demand, cost twice as much per hour and were not willing to work in our homes, especially at night, when they could get work in hospitals. But because of the new regulation, we would have to not only let our RPNs go but also lay off additional staff to offset the increased rates of the RNs. To add salt to the wound, if we were not able to fulfil our 24/7 RN coverage, we would be found noncompliant with the new regulation. In my opinion, there was little benefit to this change, except for a political sound bite.

At the time, I was on the board of our provincial association. I advocated strongly against this change. I met with the ministry to outline the adverse effects on our homes, and I spoke from the floor at members' meetings to great applause.

I did everything I could to prevent this change from taking effect. At every opportunity, I would let our people know the extent to which I was advocating on their behalf. I let them know at our administrator meetings; on road shows with all our team members, with RNs and RPNs alike; and during meetings with our unions. Our RPNs knew unequivocally that I valued and appreciated their role, and that I was doing all I could to serve as their voice.

Ultimately we lost this battle, and the regulation was put in place, but at least I had earned our people's respect.

That wasn't the first or last time I opposed a decision

made outside our control. Once, with the support of my colleague Elaine, we challenged—and successfully repealed—a ministry compliance order. As opposed to either Elaine or me sharing our advocacy efforts, at a team meeting, one of the administrators told her peers that she appreciated the great effort we were making to support her home. It was a beautiful affirmation and a great way to let our people know that they could count on us.

We didn't always win the day, but communicating that we were trying certainly increased their appreciation and tightened the bond between us.

When you're doing what's right and acting on behalf of your team, tell them. Don't take your advocacy efforts for granted.

COMMUNICATING WITH EMPATHY AND UNDERSTANDING

In addition to the rigors of long-term care I have already discussed, the LTC sector is constantly subjected to media scrutiny—certainly in Ontario, Canada—and at times that scrutiny can be cruel and hurtful to those working in LTC. What is not captured by the media is the dedication, passion, love, and resolve of those providing care to our residents. Several times over the years, the media has broadcast weeklong exposés, barraging the public with unrelenting negativity. These stories, intentionally or not, paint all homes, and all people working within them, with the same brush. One that insinuates we don't care.

In moments like these, I really feel for our teams, and I take it upon myself to craft messages, sometimes on social media, expressing my disappointment in and frustration about the coverage. I acknowledge how they must feel. I remind them that it is not about them and, most importantly, that we believe in them and honour their dedication, love, and compassion. Here's a sample of a message I shared on social media:

> **Bias Revealed—Hope for Change**
>
> I've been in health care for 30 years. Proudly, I've served in long-term care throughout my career. The pandemic, and the virus, has challenged our sector and our people beyond their limits. They have mustered their courage and been relentless in their resolve. They've worked doubles and all hours to serve and protect our residents. They've compromised their personal well-being, isolated from family as they became infected, and returned as soon as they could to do all they could to support their peers and residents.
>
> It disheartens me to see the media's sympathy for the recent and increasing pressures on hospital staff.
>
> Let's be clear, I acknowledge and applaud our peers in the hospital and the

pressures they are under in Wave 3. It is daunting and exhausting. We understand it. Because we've lived through it in Waves 1 and 2.

The BIG difference is that we suffered through it. Our sector was scrutinized, blamed, and scorned for our response to it. No matter how hard our people worked, the heroic efforts taken, the sacrifices they made, the fear they encountered and overcame, long-term care was under siege by the media. They were cruel, accusatory, and persistent in their attacks on long-term care.

We were at the front lines of the pandemic. We were under-resourced, in a time when little was known about the virus. We were not prioritized for PPE, left to defend for ourselves when staff left in fear or became COVID positive. We did everything humanly possible to serve and protect our residents. Our people were, and are, remarkable.

As I've listened to the media coverage over the last couple of days, I'm left confused by it.

Hospital staff are honoured and empathized with. They openly acknowledge the difficulties they are experiencing.

> That they're doing all they can to meet patient need, but they are struggling. And the media tells their story, honours and rallies for them.
>
> Where was the media for our people? Why are hospitals so much "better" and worthy of praise in their eyes? It's time to change the story, to change their bias.
>
> It is my hope, as we see the other side of the pandemic, that the story will change. That long-term care, and all who work in it, are honoured, appreciated, and supported for the extents to which they care. For the length they go to serve and do what is right for our residents and each other.
>
> Long-term care serves a very important and impactful role in society. Let's hope the media can learn from the pandemic and can change their story.

I issued similar messages throughout COVID. Despite these harrowing and exhausting times, our people's commitment was nothing short of exceptional. Some lived in hotels, away from their families, to keep them and our residents safe. Many worked multiple shifts. They had to put on and take off their PPE—to say nothing of the mountain of additional COVID protocol in LTC—which added stress and slowed them down. It was almost impossible to keep up with the ever-changing rules and directives from the ministry and public health. But our people did—day in, day out. They persevered.

The messages I shared during this time were my attempts to capture their reality, honour their commitment, and show our appreciation for what they were doing to serve our residents and one another. Here's a sample of another social media post:

We Rise Above—A Reflection on 2020 and Hope for 2021

2020, a year like no other
An exceptional year and extraordinary circumstances
We dealt with and battled through the unknown
It was a predatory virus, a hidden and formidable foe
But we were stronger, more resilient. We were disciplined and determined
We persevered, kept improving and kept the virus at bay

2020, a year of endurance
The most intense and challenging year of our careers
Endless hours and untold weekends

At times feeling hopeless in our efforts to
assist our homes and peers
But finding the resolve to carry on, to keep
going, to find people through unknown
sources
To interpret the never-ending changes to
directives and guidelines
And answering calls and providing clarity at
all hours

2020, a year to be remembered
A year of heroics and unconditional service
against the odds
Of selflessness, and protecting those most
vulnerable
One of donning and doffing of PPE and
never-ending hand hygiene
For some, it was living in isolation in hotels,
apart from family
It was times of personal compromise, cour-
age, and bravery

2020 revealed our humanity, compassion,
and drive
LTC was affected immensely and in unprece-
dented ways
It was rough, emotional, and exhausting

And yet here we stand, together, united, and
strong
Formidable and unrelenting, as beacons of
hope for our people
We are remarkable, honourable, and a force
to be reckoned with

2021, a dawn of a New Year
The vaccines will take their hold and create
immunity
But until they do, we are the first line of
defense
We will remain ever vigilant, tough, and
resourceful
We will be disciplined knowing it's our
means to freedom
And when we look back, we will not say we
survived
We will stand tall, united, and proud
And know that together we can say

We Rose Above and overcame this adversary

I'm sure your sector and your people have gone through challenging times too—and if they haven't, they inevitably will. Don't let your people hang out alone on the fringes. Communicate with empathy and show you care.

THE POWER OF STORYTELLING

Storytelling is one of the most powerful, immersive People First communication tools you have at your disposal. It touches hearts and minds, brings initiatives to life, and helps audiences visualize the faces of those leading change and striving for tangible outcomes.

Storytelling is a call to action, a demonstration of possibilities, an invitation for others to try something similar or perhaps do it better. Master storytelling and you'll possess a mighty instrument of engagement, one that will move you and your team toward your higher purpose and aspirations more quickly.

In my experience, the key to effective storytelling is to describe the situation before an initiative is launched—the limitations or challenges people experience—and how life is better as a result of its progress or completion.

I'm reminded of an annual three-day camping trip taken by about twenty residents at one of our homes. They stay overnight and enjoy life outdoors with their peers and team members. I have a picture of Georgina, at ninety-five years of age, sitting in a canoe for the first time in her life. That's right, ninety-five years old and she still has the sense of wonder and play to try something new. In the photo, Georgina is in a canoe with Bella and Tyler, our team members. Each of them is laughing so hard, with one of those genuine belly laughs full of excitement and exhilaration. They're having the time of their lives.

I still smile when I think of that picture. And it aligned beautifully with our Social/Recreational Initiatives Pillar and our mission to "provide happier, healthier, more fulfilling life experiences." A whole story, captured in this one photo.

At another home, Kerry-Kay, the food and nutrition manager, inadvertently ordered a "bushel" of bananas, instead of a "bunch." A bushel is a lot of bananas. What do you do with so many bananas? You make banana bread. Together with the recreation team, residents rolled up their sleeves and got to work. It was all hands on deck, both staff and residents alike having fun. Everyone participated, and most importantly our residents got to eat their own warm, handmade banana bread. The moment aligned nicely with our Dining Experience Pillar.

Steven's story was particularly memorable. One of our younger residents, Steven lived at White Eagle. Always willing to help and assume more responsibility, he was very active in the home. He was president of the residents' council, an advocate for his fellow residents, a master hand sanitizer, and the front-door greeter. His glass was always half-full, and he brought light into the lives of anyone visiting, me included.

Steven was intrigued with IMAGINE, our new dementia strategy. He would speak to the participants, ask questions, and learn as much as he could. He became an ambassador for all things IMAGINE.

I knew I had to get Steven to our national conference.

Achievable

I was representing LTC—which, again, had long been an afterthought and underdog—and wanted to make our platform proud. Together with my team, especially Brenda, my HR business partner, we devised a plan to get Steven to the convention in Chicago, where we would honour him for his interest and enthusiasm for IMAGINE.

Brenda led the charge. Steven relied on a heavy motorized wheelchair, and he would need the assistance of one of our team members. Brenda tried the airlines to no avail. They couldn't accommodate the wheelchair. She tried bus services, but the travel time was too long. But what about a helicopter? That could work. It would get Steven to Chicago and back in a day.

We had a plan. I would conduct my presentation, and toward the end I would invite Steven to join me on the stage. It was going to be incredible. We went over it with Steven. He was over the moon and could hardly contain himself.

Unfortunately, just before the conference, Steven's Nona, his grandmother, became quite ill. She was near and dear to him, and he wanted to be by her side. This was just one more reason we all loved him so much. Facing an opportunity of a lifetime, involving a helicopter no less, he instead prioritized his family.

We knew the Chicago appearance still meant the world to Steven, so we arranged to have him livestreamed on the mega-screens in front of four hundred leaders.

Onstage, I spoke about LTC's operating conditions and how our homes and leaders Rise Above these circumstances and demonstrate what is possible. I shared pictures of initiatives from each of our homes, identified individuals by name, and explained why each image was significant. Our team sat proud. I had been able to remind the audience why we served and the difference we made. Many attendees became emotional—amazed and appreciative of their LTC peers' efforts.

And at that exact moment we streamed Steven live. You could have heard a pin drop. Though nervous, Steven smiled ear to ear. He was beaming. I introduced him to the audience and had the cameras pan the room so that Steven could see how many people were there to honour him. He was awestruck. I acknowledged his dedication to his Nona and let the audience know that he would have been there in person had she been in good health.

"What do you think of the IMAGINE program?" I asked him.

"It's making life better for me and my fellow residents."

Andre, our administrator, and Dora, our program manager, were with Steven back in Toronto. I told the audience that given Steven's enthusiasm for IMAGINE, we were going to honour him as Chartwell's inaugural resident IMAGINE ambassador.

He was ecstatic. His body language and facial expression captured the room.

Andre and Dora presented him with an IMAGINE vest, and the audience rose to their feet—a standing ovation, not a dry eye in the room. Four hundred people were breathless and in awe of this young man. They had been touched. They had experienced the light Steven brings into the lives of others. It's a memory we'll never forget.

Storytelling was instrumental in enabling our platform to Rise Above, and it was one important component of our overall People First communications strategy. While I used stories in my presentation, our leaders used them in meetings, Team Ups, and town halls. It was, among many other factors, a means to focus on and acknowledge work done well. And it engaged our people and moved us toward the culture we desired.

CHAPTER 7

Overcoming Resistance

You can't move forward or make progress with people who are holding you back.

At this stage in your People First journey, most of the resistance you thought you would encounter will have diminished considerably. Up till now, I've wanted you to focus on and prioritize those team members who are doing good work and making a difference, not those resisting change. That's why this is one of the final chapters, the next-to-last concentric circle in the book. I wanted you to build momentum and your confidence before you got here. I wanted you to see in short order that you can Rise Above your circumstances.

Achievable

After all, you're now present, bringing good energy, serving as an example, and acknowledging work done well. You've set a vision and aspirational goals that engage and excite your people. And you've upped your communications game. Your team can see and feel the difference. They're letting their guard down. They're starting to believe.

You're intentionally giving more time and attention to those team members who do good work and make a meaningful difference—the ones we ordinarily take for granted, who go unnoticed, not those who present challenges or resist change.

It's important that you surround yourself with these believers, these supporters. They're the ones on board with the new direction, the ones excited about the new vision and aspirational goals. They want this change too and are prepared to support you through it. They're your ambassadors and influencers encouraging others to join your cause and build your base of support. You don't have to do all the heavy lifting. Continue to engage, enable, and empower these team members and influencers who have the respect of their peers—similar to our team that identified and empowered PSWs to become IPAC leads to stop the spread of COVID.

Just as they support you, support them. As mavericks and trailblazers, they get tired too. So check in with them regularly, ensure they're doing OK, and give them the support, coaching, and encouragement they need. Remind them what's in it for them and how their efforts align with the mission and make their own lives better. Be sure they're comfortable asking for support, seeking clarity, or making suggestions for improvement.

You don't want those leading the change to burn out. You need them, and by walking with them you'll give them the energy and endurance they need to keep going.

CONSISTENCY AND PERSEVERANCE

Change takes time.

To overcome or minimize resistance, you—and your most stalwart supporters—must demonstrate your commitment to the new vision and goals over the long haul. Dispel the notion that your renewed direction is just another flavour of the month.

You already know that not all team members are going to jump in at the same time. There's a strong likelihood that your younger and newer team members will be the first to engage in the new direction. Many of those with longer tenure will reserve their commitment and enthusiasm until they know the new changes are working and are more effective.

Being present and acknowledging work done well is never more important than now. The moment you stop or lessen your presence, the higher the probability you'll start to lose some of your people who are sitting on the fence. You may even lose some of those who joined you initially.

To build momentum, to witness meaningful change, you have to be consistent and persistent.

You have to stay strong over time. Surrounding yourself with supporters will help maintain the momentum. You'll be there for them, and they'll be there for you in those moments when you're feeling pressure to resort to the old way.

When I began my People First journey at Chartwell and changed the focus from looking for fault to work done well, it was met with some cynicism. In fact, I would go so far as to say some thought of my direction as fluffy and ungrounded.

However, I had been there before and knew what to expect. While some would think of it as a breath of fresh air, others would consider it wishful thinking. Regardless, I knew I had to convince my directors, administrators, managers, and team members that this was a better way. One that was more purposeful, engaging, and fulfilling.

Every time we got together, I would focus on and acknowledge *their* good work. I would consistently reference Rising Above and our aspirational goals. I'd ask about their initiatives on the 4 Pillars of WOW and would remind them that 85 to 90 percent of our people's work was done well and to celebrate it accordingly. I was consistent and persistent.

Here's the thing: we never stopped being compliant. Far from it. Our compliance improved. Why? Because our people were more engaged. They could see the improvements we'd made for our residents, and they were more intentional and attentive to the ministry's expectations.

Over time, your commitment to your higher purpose and aspirational goals will persuade more of your people to join you on your journey. They'll enjoy the new focus. Fence-sitters will become believers and grow your base of support.

You see, most resistors aren't intentionally rocking the boat. Rather, they're clinging to the safe harbour, to practices that are familiar to them (even if not effective or empowering). They're probably a little scared of the unknown or wondering how they're going to do their work in a new and unfamiliar environment. But once they start to see their peers do it, do it consistently, and see that it works better, they'll be more willing to give it a try. Know that most of your people just need a little more time to see the new system working, and perhaps a little more encouragement to give it another try. They too want a more meaningful and fulfilling work experience.

So be consistent and persistent. Stay the course. Know that most fence-sitters and resistors will join you with time.

HARMONY PROMOTES PROGRESS

When I first joined Chartwell, I met with my directors and platform consultants often. Our core group comprised six directors including myself, and the larger group had more than twenty internal consultants. I wanted to determine the team's synergy, the fluidity with which they worked. I wanted to know how much respect they had for one another. It became clear that there was a climate of turf protection, and some definitive lines had been drawn between operations and consulting. The director group had its own friction too.

Each individual had earned their position. They had talent, and each was capable and competent in their area of expertise. But some worked in silos, independent of others. My expectation was that they would work harmoniously, as one cohesive team. To accomplish this, I aimed to unite the group behind the mission and vision, and I emphasized that by working together we could get there more quickly.

I started with the director group. They reported directly to me. In our weekly meetings we discussed each of our homes and platform priorities. One director dominated the discussion and spoke over others.

Instead of addressing her behaviour directly, I asked everyone for their opinion. When the group was at odds—usually when this one individual wanted her way, because she was used to getting it—I would go around the table, solicit opinions, and work toward consensus. If unable to do so, I would take a vote and move forward with the ideas that garnered the greatest support. My team came to understand my expectation: if you're going to sit at our table, you're expected to voice your opinion.

When everyone had an equal voice, no one dominated. Those that previously felt undermined, intimidated, or suppressed started rising to the occasion. Their voices heard and their opinions considered, they recognized we were building cohesion.

At the platform meetings with our larger group, which included the consultants as well as the directors, I had the same objective of creating harmony. But here again, that same director dominated too much of the conversation, and few were prepared to offer alternate opinions in her presence. As before, I would let this individual know that we had heard her thoughts, and then intentionally call on others for theirs. The team was watching. I could see their spirits lighten as I respectfully asked for thoughts from other team members. They, too, came to know that everyone's opinion mattered.

Soon the domineering director started looking for and then secured a position elsewhere. She knew that my approach was inclusive and that I'd continue to solicit others' opinions. She didn't like that she had lost control and influence. Her departure opened the door to opportunities for others to flourish, spread their wings, participate actively, and work in harmony.

WORKING RESPECTFULLY WITH UNIONS

As you may recall, we had twenty-seven homes and more than fifty collective agreements with our unions. Our labour relations team was constantly in arbitrations or negotiations. As we instilled throughout our platform, how we showed up mattered. How we worked with other departments, divisions, and each other mattered. We wanted to send a message to everyone that we dealt with and whoever represented the LTC platform that we were all on the same journey. We wanted to maintain a strong collaborative relationship with our unions before and after negotiations had completed. We needed the team negotiating on our behalf to be collegial, not confrontational. Although the team negotiating on our behalf did not report to our platform, we expected them to honour the role of the union and conduct themselves in accordance with the company values.

We learned that one of the individuals representing us was becoming controversial and argumentative. She raised her voice at the union and stormed out of rooms, and her conduct was being witnessed by our administrators and union stewards. Her actions were impeding the administrator's ability to develop respectful relationships with their stewards upon return to their homes.

When we heard of this behaviour, my HR business partner spoke with the individual and reminded her of our expectations and the impact her actions had on our relationship with the union.

Unfortunately the behaviour did not subside, so we parted ways.

As long as we tolerate poor behaviour, we limit our ability to flourish, to reach our higher purpose. Your people who do good work want to make a difference. They want to contribute to a culture that's appreciative, progressive, and respectful. People who don't carry their weight, do the minimum to get by, or breed negativity in the workplace limit the growth and contribution of others. If their behaviour goes unaddressed, the people who do good work will lose hope, become discouraged, or worse, leave your organization.

CURIOSITY AND EMPATHY

Despite your best efforts, applied consistently over time, some resistors may persist.

When meeting with resistors, do it one-on-one. Groups tend to feed off each other and bolster their opposition to change. Be curious and open-minded. Try to empathize with how they feel about the changes. Position yourself so you can best understand their reasons for resisting.

You see, when you're curious, you can't be judgmental or biased. Resistors may have legitimate concerns and anxieties. Maybe they're apprehensive about not completing all their tasks. Maybe they pride themselves in being efficient and completing everything in their shift and see the new process as chaotic and slowing them down. Or maybe they've previously seen new initiatives tried and failed. "We've done this before," they might say. "It didn't work then, so why would it now?"

Your job is to listen with the intent to understand, not to comment or provide solutions. At least, not until you know the underlying reasons why they hold the positions they do.

Once you understand their perspective, you can explain the reasons for the change and how they might take small steps toward it. If they persist in saying that they've tried it before and it didn't work, outline why this time is different. Explain your higher purpose and aspirational goals and highlight how their fellow team members are embracing the changes and having success with them. Once you've reviewed everything, ask the team member if they're willing to give it another try. Let them know that their teammates are counting on them. Agree to check in once in a while to see how it's going for them. Go through this process with your other resistors.

You'll find that many just want to be heard. They want to express their concern with the process, or perhaps suggest a different way. I've found that creating this opportunity for others to express themselves, responding to their concerns, and committing to check in goes a long way toward opening the door for them to give the new process another try.

PREPARING FOR DIFFICULT CONVERSATIONS

You've come a long way. You've circumvented much of the resistance you had thought you would encounter. Most of your people have bought in or are buying in.

Predictably, some team members may not convert or share your vision. They have influence and can persuade others not to follow the new path. They can be argumentative, assertive, even aggressive. They make you feel uncomfortable. You may not feel like you have the ability to take these people on.

I've had to work with many of these individuals over my career, be they leaders, managers, or frontline team members.

Let's say you have an individual who brings negative energy to the workplace. Any time they are working, they bring others down. Morale plummets. Team members don't like it, bring it to your attention, and need you to address the behaviour.

I've learned that the better prepared I am for such a meeting, the better it goes. In this circumstance I would get as much information as I could about their behaviour, including their tone and body language. I'd find out about the frequency of the behaviour and whether it is targeted at specific team members. I'd ask how long it's been going on. I'd look at any records of similar behaviour in the past, and the expectations outlined to correct it. I'd also determine their seniority, or years of service.

Achievable

The day or night before the meeting, I play devil's advocate. I think about how the resistor will react, envisioning their body language, their facial expressions, and the arguments they might present. I determine how I'll position the discussion, how they might respond and react, and how I'll manage each of these scenarios.

Then I'll think about how I'm going to start the discussion. I want my tone to be calm and composed. Nonconfrontational. I want my body position to be open. I don't cross my arms and don't lean forward on my desk. These would convey an assertion of power and a message that I've already made up my mind.

Before I invite the individual into my space, I'll take the opportunity to centre myself. As I open the discussion, I'll start with some pleasantries and ask how they're doing and perhaps ask about their family. Afterward, I'll let them know that some concerns have been brought to my attention about their behaviour and how it makes others feel. (This is really important. It's not about them, it's about their behaviour.) I could say that their behaviour makes others feel intimidated, talked over, ignored, or belittled. I represent what has been described to me. Once I've gone over the impact of the individual's behaviour, I empathize with them and say, "It's not easy to hear."

At this point I'll ask them for their perspective. Can they imagine why their colleagues feel the way they do? They might acknowledge that they're loud and opinionated. They might go so far as to say, "I'm no-nonsense and just tell people to mind their own business and get on with their own work." They might say, "I don't believe in the new practices and I refuse to use them." They could explain that they're exhausted and irritable.

"Tell me more," or "Help me understand," I might say to get greater clarity. Again, seek to understand. That way, the individual is more likely to let down their guard.

Once I get to a position of understanding, I'll paraphrase what I've heard. I'll include the person's reasons for their own behaviour and then reiterate how it presents itself and makes others feel. I'll also confirm that it's not OK to leave others feeling the way they do. I'll look to the individual to confirm that I've accurately captured the essence of the matter.

Assuming we come to this understanding, I will ask how we might move forward. "What can you do differently to improve the feeling on the unit when you're working?" I might ask. Or "What needs to change to get us to a better place?"

"I can lower my voice and listen to others," they might say. Or "I could be more aware of the way I come across to others and change if I see adverse reactions." Or "I need to be more open-minded about the changes and look at how they make life better."

Achievable

Should we agree on an amicable solution, I'll let them know that I'm *counting on them* to do as they said. That if they do, their life will be better, as well as the lives of those they work with.

A quick note on the phrase "I'm *counting on you.*" I use this as opposed to "I'll hold you accountable." It implies that I believe in them and their commitment to do as they say they're going to do. It's a strong emotive commitment. It's not authoritative, but it sets a high personal expectation and obligation to deliver on a promise. And it works.

When closing the meeting, I'll let them know that if I don't see the behaviour change as agreed, we'll need to get back together and discuss alternate measures.

The more you prepare for these difficult conversations, the better off you'll be. It will allow you to get in the right frame of mind to think about your tone and body language, to be open and inviting and curious. These precepts will make it easier for everyone. The meeting need not be controversial and argumentative; it's about getting to a place of understanding and moving forward.

TOUGH LOVE

Invariably, some conversations with resistors will be tougher.

Let's assume you've done all the prep work and you've gone into the meeting open-minded, curious, and unbiased. You go through the pleasantries, and the individual you're meeting with just sits there with crossed arms and a frown. He's not willing to engage.

That's OK, because when playing devil's advocate you anticipated this scenario. You've reset and centred yourself, you've decided to show up fully and be your best self, and you're not going to let yourself get flustered.

As in the example before, you lay out the concerns brought to your attention by his peers and how he makes them feel. You ask if he is aware of how his behaviour is affecting others.

"I'm just doing my job," he says. "I'm here to work and that's what I do."

"Are you aware," you ask, "of how you make others feel?"

"I don't care."

"I care," you can say. "I care about how everyone feels, and I care about the culture we're working toward. It's a culture of respect and appreciation for each other and the work we do together."

"You don't have a good culture here," he might say. "These new things you're trying to do won't work. Nobody believes in them."

He's saying this to be hurtful and get under your skin. But you won't let him. You've anticipated this, and you're going to stay calm and composed.

"Your peers believe in our new direction," you could say. "They want it and are prepared to do what it takes to get there." Mention the progress the team has made and include an example or two. You can then ask if he's willing to make the changes necessary to work respectfully and in collaboration with his peers.

At this point he knows he has two choices. Either he agrees to change and join everyone on the new path, in which case you can delve into what he needs to change and come to agreement on it. Or he'll continue to stand his ground without remorse and no acknowledgment of a need to change his behaviour.

If it's the latter, state that you've brought the behaviour to his attention and offered the opportunity to change, and that he's unwilling to change and meet your expectations. Confirm that you're at a crossroads and that you'll get back to him tomorrow with your decision on the future of his employment. You could also confirm that you'll be letting him go in this meeting if you feel that's more appropriate.

People First organizations exercise tough love. They make decisions in the best interests of their people who do good work for the organization. It's about doing the right thing, not what's easy. By removing toxic individuals, you are freeing your workplace, enabling your team to live into their potential, and sending a strong message about your high standards and expectations.

If he's unwilling to change, keeping this individual will erode your culture and send the message that poor behaviour is tolerated. Your people will think that you don't care enough about them to do what is necessary and right to rid the workplace of these individuals. Without addressing this behaviour, your people who do good work will become disenfranchised, or even look for a workplace with a better culture.

If you work in a unionized environment, you might think this is not possible. Won't the union defend the employee and limit your ability to rid the workplace of these individuals?

I've worked in unionized environments throughout my career, and I can assure you that it can and should be done. No team member should have to endure the suffering imposed by bullying, humiliation, or harassment. Depending on your jurisdiction, you can terminate on a "without cause" basis, which falls outside most collective agreements. In Canada, you'll pay the individual in accordance with common-law practices that take into consideration their years of service. This is often expensive, with long tenure, but the terminations are upheld.

To me, there is no choice. Doing the right thing is the only choice. It'll be the right choice for you, your people, and your organization. It will cost money, but having a toxic workplace will cost more in lost productivity, poor performance, increased absenteeism, and staff turnover.

It will be your responsibility to advocate for termination with your superiors. Your team is counting on you, and the organization, to do the right thing.

CHAPTER 8

Dare to Be

There's nothing more powerful than a humble person, with a warrior spirit, who fights for a greater cause.

—Author unknown

One of my colleagues shared this quote with me when I was at Chartwell in the midst of the pandemic's first wave.

I've had the benefit of working with many humble leaders with warrior spirits—passionate, driven, inspirational leaders. Leaders who are empathetic, caring, and kind. Leaders who give a damn, who do the right thing. Leaders who stand with their people. Leaders who are prepared to be vulnerable and to embrace the challenges ahead of them.

I witnessed many of these traits in our leaders during COVID. They had warrior spirits. They were humble, they listened, they were present. They were proud of their people. They led with passion and conviction. They were relentless. They would not give in to the virus. They overcame it, with and for their people and their residents. The pandemic was an exceptional time that called for exceptional leaders.

Christina was one such leader. Her home had a challenging outbreak, where many of her residents and staff tested positive. They were working closely with a health unit and the Local Health Integration Network (LHIN), which added another layer of accountability and stress to the team.

Unfortunately, Christina became COVID positive. Instead of isolating at home, she quarantined in a hotel, away from her husband and young child. She was doing all she could to coordinate the efforts of the home, liaise with the corporate office, the health unit, and LHIN, and help with our recruitment efforts, all from the confines of her hotel room.

To say these were stressful and emotional days would be an understatement. It was a long outbreak, characterized by an extraordinary degree of external oversight and a new focus on infection prevention and control protocols. Christina's team was at the forefront of conducting over one hundred micro-audits a day, tabulating the results and sharing them with her team and outside agencies. It was a colossal effort. But Christina stood strong, persevered, and was determined to reach the other side of the outbreak. She led with courage and optimism, constantly reassuring her team that together they would get through the outbreak. She, like so many others, had that warrior spirit.

WE RISE ABOVE

It's easy to stand with the crowd. There's safety in numbers: you can blend in, avoid being singled out. But if you've read this book, that's not you. You have the courage of your convictions, and by now—if I've succeeded—you fully realize the impact of putting People First and becoming a People First leader.

I suspected I'd become one toward the end of my OMNI tenure, but it wasn't until 2019, when at Chartwell I was awarded Executive of the Year out of forty of my peers, that I knew my team and I had truly arrived.

At Chartwell's 2019 conference, our people were elated. Long familiar with receiving less recognition than the organization's retirement homes and general managers, our administrators noticed a change. Less than two years into my leadership role, our team was making notable strides in all our matrix including net operating income, resident satisfaction, employee engagement, and quality indicators. Together, as a platform, we were turning the tide, Rising Above, living into our 4 Pillars of WOW, and delivering on our mission. We were being recognized for our performance and moving the needle on our culture. We were getting noticed and acknowledged. We were standing taller.

I had the opportunity to make a thirty-minute presentation to the four hundred attendees. I outlined that we had five thousand team members, more than fifty collective agreements, six hundred rules and regulations to abide by; had regular ministry inspections where they only looked for fault; and were under constant assault by the media. I opened the eyes of the retirement general managers to the operating reality that our administrators and their teams had to overcome. Despite all this, I said, we were Rising Above. I presented pictures from each of our homes, identified each of the residents and team members by name, and told the stories of why the pictures were significant.

The audience was silent. Everyone was fixated on the stories of successes achieved under such challenging operating circumstances. Our administrators and our corporate team were glowing. They were finally getting the recognition they deserved. Their retirement peers were in awe. LTC was no longer an afterthought.

After the ceremonies, I learned that many of the general managers, who had not realized the difficulty of LTC's operating conditions, were acknowledging our team's accomplishments. We left that conference on a high. It gave our team the fuel to keep striving higher.

The 2020 national conference was the pinnacle of our success in long-term care. We had two full years under my leadership. Our resident survey "very satisfied" score had increased by 15 percent in two years and our employee "very engaged" score by 7.5 percent over the same period, and we were gaining ground on our retirement peers. We were better than the provincial average on all six quality indicators, our compliance record with the ministry was far better than the provincial average, and our financial performance met or exceeded every corporate target set for us. Each home had multiple initiatives on the 4 Pillars of WOW.

We had just launched IMAGINE . . . Living Life to Your Potential, our dementia strategy, and had graduated 750 frontline personal support workers from our four-day off-site program. The reaction from the participants was incredible. They were returning to their homes energized and empowered. Our platform was firing on all cylinders.

At that conference, more of our homes won awards, and our VP of finance for LTC was named Executive of the Year. (Two years in a row now, LTC executives had won this esteemed award.) The CEO and senior executives personally referenced the progress and programs in LTC. They were reciting Rising Above the Regs, IMAGINE, and the 4 Pillars of WOW. The programs had become renowned throughout Chartwell. Not only were our people glowing with pride, but we could see and feel the pride in our executives and those at the conference.

We had earned our place at the podium.

It was at this conference that I introduced Steven, livestreamed him to the audience, and honoured him as our inaugural resident IMAGINE ambassador. He had everyone, even the cameraman, in tears. We just kept raising the bar. We demonstrated what was possible, even under exceptional operating circumstances. We were no longer constrained by regulations, only by our imaginations. And we had big dreams and aspirations to live into. The more we did, the more we believed was possible. And IMAGINE—the catalyst that would catapult us into a different orbit—was just getting started.

Unfortunately, one month later, in March 2020, the World Health Organization declared COVID-19 a pandemic. However, the momentum we had created and the improvements in our culture and communication we had accomplished in these two years helped carry us through it. COVID never stopped us from looking for and acknowledging work done well. In fact, acknowledging it was never more important.

At our virtual conference in February 2021, we did not have survey results to review. We had halted data collection during COVID. But I was able to conduct a couple of brief sessions. One was titled "And Still, We Rise Above." The session's description read: "Challenged by a formidable and invisible foe, COVID-19 tested our mettle, courage, and character. As we do in LTC, we Rise Above. We gathered our collective strength, we fought long and hard, never gave up, persevered, and overcame."

As I had in prior sessions, I described the circumstances and impact that the virus had on our residents and people. I spoke to their courage and conviction. I honoured those who were living out of a hotel to protect the health and safety of our residents. I thanked them for their relentless efforts and selfless commitment to overcoming the virus. And of course, I showed pictures from each LTC home that captured heroic efforts, endless love, and exceptional kindness under such trying circumstances. This time, instead of speaking alongside the picture presentation, I played "Rise Up" by Andra Day. An emotional track, it spoke to the ache and exhaustion of our people and how they themselves would Rise Up time and again.

What we did together in long-term care was remarkable. Against the odds, we demonstrated that you can Rise Above your circumstances. Through the strategies I've shared with you in this book, we made believers of our people and those watching from the sidelines.

NOW IS YOUR TIME

You've started on a journey to improve lives, including your own. You've learned about the power of putting People First. You're going to engage the hearts and minds of your people by focusing on, and acknowledging, work done well. They'll feel the difference, as will you.

If you do nothing else other than focus on and acknowledge work done well, your life and the lives of those you lead will be better.

But you're not going to stop there.

You're on a mission to Rise Above and create a culture of possibility and potential. You're going to keep building on that momentum. You'll set and share your vision and aspirational goals. You'll change the way you lead and incorporate people-focused communication. You know the more you acknowledge your people, the more engaged they'll become, the more initiatives they'll undertake, and the more progress you'll make. And most of your resistors will become believers. Heck, they may even become your greatest champions.

It's going to be an incredible journey.

Dare to be who you're capable of being. Let go of your inhibitions. The only person holding you back is yourself.

You've got the passion. You've got the potential. And now you have the tools to live into it. Be that life-giving, inspirational leader who demonstrates what's possible when you engage, enable, and empower your people.

A Final Thought

It's my hope that you've found the answers you were looking for within the covers of *Achievable*. That it's left you feeling confident, inspired, and motivated to create a culture of possibility and potential.

This book is intentionally short, simple, and understandable. It's achievable. It's a solution that will move the needle on the disengagement epidemic . . . if you choose to put the teachings into practice.

It's so short that it could lift your spirits and lighten your load—but just for a day or two, like a keynote speech. The kind of speech that makes people feel good in the moment, but that most people do nothing with. You could read this book and then go about life as usual and continue to face your daily grind and mountain of paperwork.

Or you can decide to change your mindset and commit to putting your People First, getting on the floor, and acknowledging their work done well. Do that and you'll improve your life and the lives of those you lead. Do that—witness its impact, feel the difference—and you'll want to follow the next steps laid out in the book.

As a reminder, when you set a higher purpose, you're taking the first steps toward living a bigger life. One where you feel more alive because you've committed to something bigger, something better.

Make the choice to live a bigger, better life. It's yours for the taking. It's time to get started.

Acknowledgments

This book would not have been possible without my dad. He was my greatest mentor and biggest fan. He believed in me and provided me with opportunities to grow and the autonomy to spread my wings, and he empowered me to act in the best interests of our company. While he was great with numbers, I became great with people. Together, we were a dynamic duo.

There are many people who have my thanks for their help making this book a reality:

To my mum for her unconditional love and belief that I could do anything I set my mind to.

To my wife, Deb, for her loving critique of the book. You always find a supportive way to make what I do better. To my daughter Ainsley for your creative input on the book cover, website, and business-card design. Your insights and influence elevated each one of them. And to my daughter Chelsea for being my soundboard and audience when I practice my speeches.

To my brother, Grant, who bought me *It's Your Ship* and had it signed by Captain Michael Abrashoff. His book was instrumental in transitioning our people from managers to leaders at both OMNI and Chartwell.

To Karen Sullivan for your leadership and unwavering support and advocacy for our LTC platform. You were always responsive to our needs and empowered me, and our team, to do what was necessary to drive change within our platform.

To Brenda (Prieur) McGuirk, my friend, colleague, and HR business partner. You were my strategist, advocate, and supporter who kept pushing me to do more and be more for our people. I'm indebted to you for your encouragement to write this book.

To my directors and consultants whom I worked with and walked beside, I thank you for your passion, dedication, and commitment to improving the lives of those we served. Together we demonstrated that we can, and should, rise above our daily challenges and demonstrate what's possible.

To Lisa Smith, the champion of all things IMAGINE. You brought this incredible dementia strategy to life for all those who participated in it. You immersed yourself completely and encapsulated all of the teachings of this book. You stand as a beacon of hope and inspiration for those who serve in long-term care.

To Deb Bakti, a fellow author, for sharing your writing experiences and for giving me the fuel that kept me on track while writing the book.

To my writing coach and mentor AJ Harper and her dean of students Laura Stone. I had no appreciation of the amount of time, effort, and resolve that were needed to write a book. Your book *Write a Must Read*, the Top Three Book Club, and your writing community made the writing experience immersive, experiential, and tenable. Together, you were the gift that kept on giving through the writing of the book.

To my team at Girl Friday Productions, thank you. I extend a special thanks especially to Mari Kesselring, publishing manager; Georgie Hockett, marketing specialist; and Matt Patin, developmental editor, for investing you time, energy, and expertise in my book.

And finally, to all of you who have taken the time to read *Achievable*, it is my hope that it enables you, and your people, to live a better life, do more of the work you love, and demonstrate what's possible.

About the Author

Fraser Wilson's personal motto is "Making others more," and it's the reason he wrote *Achievable.* Wilson knows from experience what it takes to be a leader who inspires and motivates people in a sector that is heavily regulated, overscrutinized, underfunded, and chastised by the media.

Both at OMNI Health Care and at Chartwell Retirement Residences' long-term care platform, Wilson inspired his people to rise above their daily demands and challenges, engaging, enabling, and empowering them to live into their potential, and demonstrated what's possible.

Wilson was owner and CEO of OMNI Health Care, which had sixteen long-term care homes and 1,500 employees. He sold it in 2007 to a private equity firm impressed by its culture, brand, and financial performance. In 2017, Wilson joined Chartwell Retirement Residences as vice president of long-term care operations, where he was responsible for twenty-seven homes and five thousand employees. Under his leadership, his platform won awards within the company and the sector. His team also accomplished a 15 percent increase in residents' "very satisfied" score and a 7.5 percent increase in employees' "very engaged" score in two years. In his second year with Chartwell, Wilson was awarded Executive of the Year.

Wilson served on the board of directors of the Ontario Long Term Care Association for more than fifteen years and has been its chair. Today, he speaks at conferences to businesses and their leaders about creating a culture of possibility and potential based on the strategies laid out in *Achievable.*